Nine Investments Abroad
and
Their Impact at Home

Nine Investments Abroad and Their Impact at Home

Case Studies on Multinational Enterprises and the U.S. Economy

ROBERT B. STOBAUGH
Professor of Business Administration
Harvard University

With the Collaboration of

Jose de la Torre, Jr.
Robert H. Hayes
James V. Jucker
Richard W. Moxon
Rita M. Rodriguez

James G. Keddie
Pedro Nueno
Jules Pogrow
Robert C. Ronstadt
Piero Telesio
Phillip L. Townsend

DIVISION OF RESEARCH
Graduate School of Business Administration
Harvard University
Boston   1976

Distributed by
Harvard University Press
Cambridge, Massachusetts
and
London, England

Library of Congress Catalog Card No. 74-20368
ISBN 0-87584-113-9

HD69
.I7S765x

Printed in the United States of America

Preface

THIS WAS A TEAM PROJECT. Even though I bear final responsibility for the book, and especially for the first chapter and the last two chapters, we all shared in the pleasures inherent in such a project—doing the field work, writing and rewriting the drafts, and participating in seminar discussions. But as someone wrote many years ago, "Pleasure is nothing else but the intermission of pain." So we shared in the pains also inherent in such a project—the tedious checking and rechecking of data and the inevitable late-night push to complete the final draft.

Though it was a team effort, each of us was responsible for one or more studies, as follows:

FOOD PRODUCTS (industry 20 in the U.S. Standard
    Industrial Classification)
        Robert B. Stobaugh and Pedro Nueno
PAPER AND ALLIED PRODUCTS (SIC 26)
        Jose de la Torre, Jr.
CHEMICALS AND ALLIED PRODUCTS (SIC 28)
        Robert B. Stobaugh and Phillip L. Townsend
PETROLEUM (SIC 29)
        Robert H. Hayes and Robert C. Ronstadt
RUBBER PRODUCTS (SIC 30)
        Rita M. Rodriguez and Jules Pogrow
PRIMARY AND FABRICATED METALS (SIC 33
    and 34)
        Jose de la Torre, Jr.
NONELECTRICAL MACHINERY (SIC 35)
        Robert B. Stobaugh and Piero Telesio
ELECTRICAL MACHINERY (SIC 36)
        Richard W. Moxon (based on a Harvard
        teaching case by Bruce McKern)

TRANSPORTATION EQUIPMENT (SIC 37)
James V. Jucker and James G. Keddie
EFFECTS ON AGGREGATE BALANCE OF PAY-
MENTS AND EMPLOYMENT
Robert B. Stobaugh and Piero Telesio
EFFECTS ON EMPLOYMENT SKILL LEVELS
Jose de la Torre, Jr., and Piero Telesio

These unpublished pieces formed the raw material from
which I wrote the text, sometimes using quite a bit from
the studies and other times using only a small fraction of
the available material.

Four members of the Department of Commerce—Daniel
Arrill, S. Stanley Katz, Charles O'Rourke, and Harold
Scott—saw the value of case studies in attempting to answer the fundamental question underlying the effect of
U.S. foreign direct investment on the U.S. balance of
payments and U.S. employment. This fundamental question is: What would have happened if the investment had
not been made? And they were responsible for the funding
which allowed the project to be undertaken.

The effort was a crash project by any standards. A
contract was signed in September 1971 between Harvard
University and the U.S. Department of Commerce, providing funds for the case studies. Four months later, in
January 1972, a summary of the results of the study was
released, and the Department published this summary two
months later as Part II of Volume 1 of *The Multinational
Corporation, Studies on U.S. Foreign Investment* (Washington, D. C.: Superintendent of Documents, March 1972).

We received help from a number of places. The multinational enterprises that we studied made available to us a
certain amount of confidential information. For this coop-
eration during a period when many of their managers were

occupied with the turmoil that followed the floating of the dollar in August 1971, we are grateful. Even though our basic description of the companies' actions and their stated reasons for these actions came from the companies, we used our best judgment in preparing all estimates appearing in this book. Thus, none of the companies necessarily agrees with either the analyses or our conclusions.

A number of persons gave us valuable comments, either at seminars or in reviewing our drafts, or both: especially Raymond Vernon, and also Gary C. Hufbauer, Donald Lessard, Thomas Horst, and three reviewers unknown to us.

Max Hall, as editorial adviser, reviewed the book manuscript. As he has done on so many occasions, he asked the seemingly simple questions that exposed incomplete analyses, illogical thoughts, or subtle inconsistencies. Whatever the book's shortcomings, there would have been a lot more without Max's help.

There are many other activities that take place behind the scenes. George Middleton, William Samuelson, and Susan Stobaugh gathered and analyzed industry data. Kathy Harlan handled many of the innumerable administrative tasks involved in such a project, and also typed a number of the studies. Madelyn Wisnia typed several drafts of the manuscript. Howard Kailes and Lauren Behrman checked the references, no easy task when so many authors were involved. And Carole Doyle, who by now is an expert in deciphering my hieroglyphics, typed the final manuscript. Eve Bamford performed the final proofreading and Ellen Kurnit edited the final manuscript. Hilma Holton was responsible for the entire production process. To all of these, I am thankful.

Finally, Richard Walton, my friend and colleague who is Director of the Division of Research, Harvard Business

School, provided the needed encouragement for me to turn the studies into a book manuscript. Financial support for this project was administered by the Division of Research of the Harvard Business School. We are deeply indebted to The Associates of the School and the U.S. Department of Commerce for their financial support.

ROBERT B. STOBAUGH

Soldiers Field
Boston, Massachusetts
March 1976

Table of Contents

*U.S. Exports of Capital Equipment . . . U.S.
Exports of Parts and Components . . . Other
U.S. Exports . . . U.S. Imports . . . U.S. Re-
ceipts of Royalties and Fees*

List of Tables

List of Figures

Nine Investments Abroad
and
Their Impact at Home

1

The Setting

THE BOARD OF DIRECTORS of one of America's large corporations sat at their long table and listened carefully as the firm's top international executive urged them to build a plant in a remote country halfway around the world.

The proposal did not go unchallenged. The chief financial officer, well stocked with figures on costs, sales, and cash flows, argued that the return on investment "just wasn't adequate" considering the risk involved.

The international executive emphasized a different view: What would happen if they didn't make the investment? To frighten his fellow executives, he conjured up evil spirits—*the competition*! And not just ordinary competition, the kind they all knew and played golf with at industry meetings, but *foreign competition*—those speaking unfamiliar tongues, obeying "no rules of the game," and constantly grasping for "our markets."

The international executive's scenario was clear: Either the company expands to keep or extend its foothold in this distant market or it eventually will lose the market and withdraw. This would hurt doubly, for it would weaken the company's worldwide position and at the same time strengthen that of the competitors. And if this pattern were repeated often enough, the competitors would even begin to take over the firm's U.S. market. Thus the international executive argued that there was no alternative but to make the investment. Such reasoning is often sufficient to deflect arguments based narrowly on financial projections. And the use of a considerable amount of judgment to resolve such questions seems appropriate, because financial projections are necessarily based on a partial analysis, with especially light treatment of the long-run competitive effects of various alternatives.

In this book on the effects of U.S. investments abroad, we, like the international executive, give much consideration to "what happens if the firm doesn't invest." But there's a difference. The international executive considers what happens *with* the investment compared with what happens *without* the investment in order to judge the effects of the investment on his firm. Here, we consider what happens *with* such investments compared with what happens *without* such investments in order to judge the effects of such investments on the U.S. balance of payments and U.S. employment.

Our studies include only foreign *direct* investment, not foreign *portfolio* investment. A direct investment is one in which the investor has control over the operations of the foreign facilities. Otherwise the capital flow is said to be a portfolio investment.

Our study, of course, is not the first on the subject; and an acquaintance with the prior works will help put ours into perspective. Since 1950 there has been a good deal of discussion as to whether foreign direct investment is good for either the home nation or the host nation—the home country being, of course, the source of the investment, and the host country being the recipient of the investment. An initial trickle of articles concerned with the welfare of the host country was followed by others showing concern for the home country.

Kennedy administration officials showed a general concern with the deficits in the U.S. balance of payments. At the same time, the U.S. Treasury Department wanted to increase taxes collected from U.S. foreign direct investors. Together these two concerns in the early 1960s served to focus attention on the balance-of-payments effects of U.S. foreign direct investment.

There began a sporadic outpouring of statements and studies, ranging all the way from pronouncements, to surveys of opinion, to simple econometric models. In 1965 the Treasury Department commissioned two economists, G. C. Hufbauer and F. M. Adler, to attempt to analyze the consequences to the U.S. balance of payments of U.S. foreign direct investment outflows in manufacturing. The scope was limited to manufacturing, because of the difficulties involved in analyzing the effect of foreign direct investment in the raw material industries.[1]

The Hufbauer-Adler study, tediously constructed with dozens of statistical analyses, was published in 1968.[2] The authors expressed their primary results in terms of *recoupment periods*, that is, the number of years required for a direct investment outflow to produce a cumulative stream of balance-of-payments inflows equal to itself. This work met an important objective in providing models with which others can work. Furthermore, it made an impor-

---

[1] For a discussion of these difficulties, see Raymond Vernon, *U.S. Controls on Foreign Direct Investment—A Reevaluation* (Financial Executives Research Foundation, 1969), pp. 61–64.

[2] G. C. Hufbauer and F. M. Adler, *Overseas Manufacturing Investments and the Balance of Payments* (Washington, D.C.: U.S. Treasury Department, 1968).

tant finding. The financial flows resulting from the trade consequences of foreign direct investment have a much greater impact on the balance of payments than do the direct financial flows, such as the initial investment outflow and subsequent receipts of dividends. Although Hufbauer and Adler studied all types of trade, including exports of capital equipment and parts and components, they found that the trade consequence of most importance is the extent to which production abroad by U.S. affiliates displaces U.S. exports. They realized that in cases in which a U.S. firm chooses to invest abroad to serve a foreign market even though it could just as well serve the foreign market by U.S. exports, then the foreign investment would cause a displacement of U.S. exports. But if the option of serving the foreign market with U.S. exports does not exist, then the foreign investment would not cause a displacement of U.S. exports.

Even though the Hufbauer-Adler work still represents by far the best econometric study of the subject, it is not adequate for policy determination; for its estimates of the results of investment abroad depend mainly upon unexplored and untested assumptions about what would have happened to U.S. exports if U.S. foreign direct investment had not taken place. The results of foreign direct investment generally are favorable to the U.S. balance of payments if one assumes that production from U.S.-owned plants abroad will not displace U.S. exports and unfavorable if one assumes that it will. Indeed, Hufbauer and Adler were so unsure of their estimates of displacement effects that they made arbitrary adjustments in order to bring their results more into line with commonly accepted notions about replacement periods.[3] Moreover, the Hufbauer-Adler model does not capture some impor-

<hr>

[3] Hufbauer and Adler, *Overseas Manufacturing Investments*, p. 67.

tant dynamic elements such as changes in physical efficiency and innovation and the subsequent effects on price;
and these are perhaps the most important factors to consider in judging the long-term effects of foreign direct
investment.[4]

At the end of the 1960s, organized labor in the United
States began an attack on U.S. foreign direct investors,
especially the big ones—the multinational enterprises. In
contrast to the dialogues concerning the balance of payments, labor's charges went beyond economic issues and
covered a wide range of alleged misdeeds—ranging from
displaying an affinity for foreign dictatorships, to dodging
taxes with secret Swiss bank accounts, to exploiting
foreign workers. But the primary charges were that U.S.
multinational enterprises exported American jobs.[5] Implicit in these accusations was the assumption that U.S.
firms could earn an adequate profit by serving markets
from U.S. facilities, but instead chose to produce abroad
to earn even higher profits. Labor's concern, unlike that of
the Hufbauer-Adler study, related to any foreign manufacturing subsidiary of a U.S. firm, whether or not it was
associated with a capital outflow from the United States;
the focus was on U.S.-owned production abroad, regard-

---

[4] For a further discussion of these issues, see Raymond Vernon, *U.S. Controls on Foreign Direct Investment—a Reevaluation*, pp. 39–64, For an indica-
tion of the possible effect of foreign production on U.S. efficiency, see Robert B.
Stobaugh, et al., *The Likely Effects on the U.S. Economy of Eliminating the
Deferral of U.S. Income Tax on Foreign Earnings* (Cambridge, Mass.: Management Analysis Center, 745 Concord Avenue, 1973), Chapter 5.

[5] For examples, see Jeff Miller, "Importation and Exploitation," *The IUE
News*, April 10, 1969, pp. 12–13; "International Trade," Report of the
Economic Policy Committee to the AFL-CIO Executive Council, mimeo-
graphed, February 1970; Lane Kirkland, "The Developing Crisis in International
Trade," an address to a conference of the Industrial Union Department of the
AFL-CIO, Sheraton Park Hotel, Washington, D.C., reprinted in *Congressional
Record*, April 16, 1970, pp. E3327–E3328.

less of where the funds were obtained. However, regardless of the definition of foreign direct investment, no analytical model, such as the Hufbauer-Adler model for balance of payments, was available to estimate the employment effects.

None of the foregoing studies, neither those dealing with balance of payments nor employment, consisted of a detailed analysis of individual investment decisions. Yet without such detailed analyses, it is impossible to estimate with any degree of satisfaction what would have happened if U.S. foreign direct investment had not taken place, for detailed studies are needed to estimate such factors as the dynamic effects of an investment and the competitive positions of U.S. firms compared with foreign firms.

Because of this void, the Harvard Business School secured the financial support of the U.S. Department of Commerce in 1971 to make the study reported in this book. The study was limited to analyses of the effects of U.S. foreign direct investment on the balance of payments and employment of the United States. It did not try to measure the effects on host countries or on other countries, such as those containing the headquarters of multinational enterprises that compete with U.S.-based multinational enterprises. This was not because those effects are unimportant, but rather because we wanted to keep the scope of our work within reasonable bounds to allow an early completion date—a summary of our results was issued less than six months after the start of the project.[6]

---

[6] Robert B. Stobaugh, et al., "U.S. Multinational Enterprises and the U.S. Economy," in Bureau of International Commerce, U.S. Department of Commerce, *The Multinational Corporation*, Volume I (Washington: Superintendent of Documents, 1972); and Robert B. Stobaugh, Piero Telesio and Jose de la Torre, Jr., *The Effect of U.S. Foreign Direct Investment in Manufacturing on the U.S. Balance of Payments, U.S. Employment and Changes in Skill Composition of Employment*, Occasional Paper No. 4, Center for Multinational Studies (Washington, D.C., February 1973).

CHARACTERISTICS OF FOREIGN DIRECT INVESTMENTS SELECTED FOR NINE CASE STUDIES

Industry from which case was selected	Subsidiary existing or new at time of study	Ownership by U.S. company	Primary market planned to be served by investment	Size of project (in millions of dollars)	Geographic location of investment	
					Developed countries	Less-developed countries
FIVE CASES DESCRIBED IN THIS BOOK						
Transportation equipment	New	Wholly owned	Local	7	—	S.E. Asia
Rubber products	Existing	Wholly owned	Local	8	Canada	—
Food products	New	Joint venture	Third countries	1	—	Africa
Electrical machinery	New	Wholly owned	U.S.	8	—	S.E. Asia
Nonelectrical machinery	Existing	Wholly owned	Local and Third countries	55	Europe	—
FOUR OTHER CASES SUMMARIZED IN THIS BOOK						
Chemicals and allied products	New and expansion	Joint venture	Local	25	Japan	—
Primary and fabricated metals	New and expansion	Wholly owned (later joint venture)	Local	5	—	Latin America
Paper and allied products	Existing	Wholly owned	Local	20	Canada	—
Petroleum	New	Wholly owned	Third countries	195	Europe[a]	—

[a] Investment also includes oil tankers.

in this book and have provided a summary of the other four in Chapter 7. To give some flavor of the logic used in selecting the five detailed cases, here are some examples. Although two investments in Canada were studied, in tires and in paper, we wanted to present only one Canadian investment. The tire case was chosen because it represented one extreme—it had the longest recoupment period of any of the nine cases, both for the balance of payments and employment. Two investments in less-developed countries made to serve the market of the host country were studied, but we wanted to present only one. The case on transportation equipment (automobiles) was selected because it was a new investment and hence more typical than the metals case, which was an acquisition of an existing facility. Furthermore, an acquisition of a foreign facility already in existence is a feature of the canned fruit case, which was selected because it illustrates an investment's serving a market in third countries; that is, the market of neither the home nor host country.

Our study focuses especially on the export displacement effects of the nine investments. The reason is simple—Hufbauer and Adler were quite unsure of their assumptions about export displacements, yet found that these assumptions affected the overall results more than any other factor.

As opposed to Hufbauer and Adler, we deliberately omitted the indirect-trade effects; that is, trade induced because of increases or decreases in general economic activity resulting from foreign direct investment. Also, we omitted the effects that would have arisen as a result of the alternative use of funds in the United States that might have occurred if the U.S. foreign direct investment had not been made. Hufbauer and Adler found these effects to be relatively small compared with other effects. In any event, the effect of foreign direct investment on the level of economic activity and investment can be offset by fiscal and monetary policy.[9]

Since the methodology in our analyses differs from that used in any prior study, the reader is entitled to an explanation of our procedures. Our study perhaps could have been entitled "what might have been." It is distinguished from all other studies by our attempt to estimate what would have happened to the U.S. balance of payments and U.S. employment if a given foreign direct investment had *not* been made. For this analysis we assumed that the market served by the facility actually built could not have been served from any other U.S.-owned facility abroad—whether owned by the firm in our case or by any other U.S. firm and whether located in the host country or a third country. The rationale for this assumption is straightforward: It is unlikely that a U.S. regulation would prevent the expansion in our case but allow other U.S.-owned expansions abroad to serve the same market.

Thus, in our "what might have been" scenario, if the market in question were to be served and if the investment in question were not made, the goods would have come from one of the following sources:

(1) Facilities in the United States, either existing or built especially for this purpose;

(2) Facilities located in the host country, either existing or built especially for this purpose, and owned by firms not controlled from the United States; or

(3) Facilities located in a third country, either existing or built especially for this purpose, and owned by firms not controlled from the United States.

Like the union spokespersons, we, too, believe that

[9] For a further discussion of this point, see U.S. Tariff Commission, *The Multinational Corporation and the World Economy* (Washington, D.C.: U.S. Government Printing Office, 1973), p. 649.

U.S. firms go abroad to earn more profits than they could earn by producing in the United States for the same markets. But, rather than adopting the unions' assumption that U.S. production would be profitable, in each case we explicitly studied the profit that the firm would earn by producing in the United States rather than abroad and then drew conclusions about the firm's likely actions.

It is obvious that our estimates rely heavily on estimates concerning the foreign competition faced by U.S. firms. Hence, in each industry, a thorough study was made of competition and patterns of investment and trade. In every case we—not the companies—are responsible for the estimates that we used, and in most cases the company has not seen our final estimates.

To obtain the net effects of the U.S. firm's expansion abroad, we subtracted the results of the "what might have been" case from our estimates of the U.S. balance of payments and employment that occurred or were expected to occur *with* the expansion. We then went further and calculated the skill levels of the person-hours of employment gained or lost as a result of each investment. In most cases the investment decision was so recent that actual results were not available at the time of our field research. In the few cases where actual results were available, they were used. By interviewing several managers having different functions within the firm, we attempted to avoid bias on matters not substantiated by records. In the remaining cases, we used company projections, usually obtained from documents prepared as part of the internal approval process, as the basis of our estimates of what would occur with the investment.

Some industry data were obtained directly from the companies studied, but mostly the data came from published sources. In a few cases, information was obtained by interviewing other firms.

In estimating the effects that a change in the level of a company's production has on the company's employment, the nature of the data makes a difference. To illustrate: if a parent company is producing 10,000 components with 1,000 person-years of work, the average production is 10 components per person-year; and if an investment abroad demands an increment of 500 components per year in the U.S. plant, the use of average data would suggest an employment increase of 50 person-years. On the other hand, the *marginal* employment needed to produce the additional 500 units might be less or more than 50 person-years, depending on the situation in the firm at that time. We ordinarily used average data and this seemed safest in terms of long-run effects. But in some instances, where marginal data were reliably known and seemed applicable to the case, we took that route. The method used in each case is indicated in the tables that contain the detailed estimates.

A jungle of assumptions and judgments supports our analyses, and an understanding of this jungle means treading a slow, tortuous path. This we do in the next five chapters, for each of the five detailed cases. But since not all estimates are of equal importance or uncertainty, we attempt to make the path easier by focusing most fully on items of greatest importance and greatest uncertainty. We found the journey interesting, not just because of balance-of-payments and employment estimates, but because these are real cases with real people.

2

Serving the Market of a Less-Developed Country: Automobile Assembly in Asiana

> The peasant village consists typically of a few dozen or a few hundred houses clustered along a single dirt street or a group of intersecting streets. . . . The typical house consists of one room. Except in cold country, the floor is the dirt of the ground . . . .
> Half of the children [that the peasant] begets die before the age of five years; or if he lives in a less favorable environment, half may die before the age of one.[1]

MOST OF THE POPULATION OF THE WORLD lives in conditions not much better than these, and nowhere are there more peasants than in Asia. The governments of most less-developed countries have sought to break this traditional pattern by creating jobs, particularly industrial jobs.

[1] Everett C. Hagen, *On the Theory of Social Change* (Homewood, Illinois: Richard D. Irwin, 1962), pp. 62, 63, 65.

And the automobile industry has been a prime field for this effort. Especially since World War II, many less-developed countries have forced importers to assemble vehicles locally, and this step has often been followed by laws requiring an increasing amount of the components to be made locally.

Concurrent with the movement toward self-sufficiency in automobile manufacture, the ownership pattern changes. Originally the importer is a local businessman who distributes the vehicles nationally, sometimes through one or more of his own retail outlets. Although the distributor might start the assembly operations, the manufacturer eventually takes over the assembly job, sometimes when local manufacture of components begins, but sometimes earlier.

One microcosm of the development of the world automotive industry is the story of Michigan Motors Corporation's (a disguised name) 1967 investment in assembly facilities in an Asian country, which we call "Asiana." Michigan Motors, a leading U.S. automotive manufacturer, began exporting to Asiana in the early 1900s. In the mid-1950s the local distributor began assembling vehicles from Michigan Motors' factories in the United States and Continental Europe. A few years later a different local distributor began to assemble vehicles made in the corporation's United Kingdom factory. The tax structure of Asiana virtually precludes the importation of assembled vehicles (Table 2-1).

These arrangements worked quite well for Michigan Motors until 1965, when the distributor assembling the U.K. vehicles began to have financial problems. Michigan Motors reacted by transferring these assembly operations to the distributor handling its vehicles made in the United States and Continental Europe. But this was not a perma-

TABLE 2-1
EFFECT OF ASIANA'S TAXES ON COST OF IMPORTED CAR
(U.S. dollars per car)

		Car assembled in	
		Europe	Asiana
Cost, delivered in Asiana, excluding import duty		1,288	1,017
Local handling costs, including customs broker		32	30
Local assembly costs		0	263
Local taxes			
Import duty	515		254
Advance sales tax	2,723		112
Manufacturer's tax	0		255
Municipal tax	2		2
Subtotal		3,240	623
Total		4,560	1,933

SOURCE: Estimates of Michigan Motors Corporation for one of its standard European cars.

nent solution because the owners of this distribution operation no longer wanted to continue their automobile business and, in fact, had been attempting to sell all of their operations so that they could retire.

At first Michigan Motors made no move to change the situation. But as the sales figures began to roll in for 1965, the head of the firm's Asian and African operations (a section of the International Division), whom we call by the disguised name of John Adams, decided that something had to be done. In that year the firm's share of the Asiana market in cars and trucks was 19 percent, down from 28 percent in 1964; it had not fallen below 23 percent during the prior seven years. Furthermore, for the first time, it dropped substantially below that of Michigan Motors' main competitor, another leading U.S. automotive manufacturer that assembled vehicles locally. (Table 2-2). In addition, Japanese companies had increased their market share from 4 percent to 26 percent in the last four years.

TABLE 2-2
MARKET SHARE OF CARS AND TRUCKS IN ASIANA:
MICHIGAN MOTORS CORPORATION AND ITS
LEADING U.S. COMPETITOR, 1958–1965
(*percent*)

	1958	1959	1960	1961	1962	1963	1964	1965
Michigan Motors Corp.	24	28	30	25	24	23	28	19
Leading U.S. competitor	22	18	20	17	22	24	23	23
Total	46	46	50	42	46	47	51	42

SOURCE: Company records.

To many businessmen the loss of market share has the same effect as the prospect of a hangman's noose in the morning: it concentrates the mind.[2] In the case of Michigan Motors, John Adams concluded that the loss of market share was due to the lackadaisical efforts of the local distributor-assembler. He further concluded that the only viable alternative was for Michigan Motors to purchase and operate the assembly operations in Asiana; apparently there were no other companies willing to purchase and operate these facilities, for the local distributor had not been able to sell his operation.

Adams and his staff moved quickly. They negotiated a purchase price for the assembly facilities of the local distributor and obtained an estimate of the funds needed to

---

[2] This was paraphrased from "Depend upon it, sir, when a man knows he is to be hanged in a fortnight, it concentrates his mind wonderfully." Samuel Johnson, *Epitaph on Goldsmith*, September 19, 1777.

convert this facility into one conforming to the standard design used overseas by Michigan Motors. Adams then launched a trial proposal through the bureaucracy that is ubiquitous in multinational enterprises.

The trial proposal met opposition from the corporate financial staff, which considered the estimated after-tax return on investment too low, especially when the political and economic risks involved in Asiana were taken into account. Such opposition was not about to sidetrack John Adams, and he was able to improve the profitability estimate for the venture.

First, he asked the engineers responsible for plant design and manufacturing methods to revise the standard design and methods used previously in other countries to see if they could reduce the investment in Asiana even though more plant labor might be required. Wages were relatively low in Asiana, approximately $1,000 per worker annually. The engineers responded with a new design and new manufacturing methods that reduced the investment in fixed assets by almost $1 million. This in turn reduced depreciation and tooling amortization more than enough to offset the costs of the additional workers. Thus, the projected profit increased, even though the amount of the investment required was lower. Although the substitution of labor for machinery would result in less consistency in the product from the assembly operations, additional handwork could be performed, giving these products the required level of quality.

The second action that Adams took to raise the return on investment was simple: he increased the projections of sales that could be made with the new facilities. He did this by eliminating one of the "safety factors" contained in his trial proposal. His staff originally had estimated that Michigan Motors would capture about 21 percent of the

Asiana market over the next ten years with the proposed investment and only 12 percent without the proposed investment, or a difference of 9 percentage points. In the trial proposal, Adams had reduced this difference to 6 percentage points. For the revised proposal he merely reinstated the 9 percentage point difference.

The revised proposal was still opposed, though not so strongly, by the corporate financial staff, which continued to point out the political and economic uncertainties, which they said "typify those of other low-volume, underdeveloped markets." In addition, they mentioned the likelihood that the volume projections would not be realized because of the strong Japanese competitors. Adams, however, with the support of International Division management, prevailed. The president of Michigan Motors approved the project and subsequently, early in 1967, the board of directors did too. A further drop in the market share to 15 percent in 1966 had helped Adams sell the proposal to the president.

The proposal called for an initial investment of $6.8 million in total assets—$4.2 million in fixed assets, plus $2.6 million in working capital in order to grant more credit to dealers. The proposal showed projected corporate profits after taxes of some $850,000 annually, for an average return after taxes of about 13 percent on total assets employed. The proposal also showed a projected payback period of four years. Michigan Motors planned to make a nominal investment in the form of equity of only $100,000. Local debts in the form of accounts payable would provide $500,000 and local borrowings another $400,000. The additional funds were to be obtained through dollar loans and through merchandise credit from the parent or sister subsidiaries, as shown in Table 2-3.

The proposal indicated that the Asiana subsidiary would

TABLE 2-3

BALANCE SHEET PLANNED FOR MICHIGAN MOTORS CORPORATION
SUBSIDIARY IN ASIANA, YEAR-END, 1967 AND 1968

(Millions of Dollars)

	1967	1968
Assets		
Cash and receivables	$ —	$ 0.3
Inventories	2.6	3.2
Net fixed assets	4.2	3.7
Total	$ 6.8	$ 7.2
Liabilities and equity		
Local payables	$ 0.5	$ 0.6
Borrowings—local	0.4	0.5
Borrowings—dollar	5.2	5.2
Merchandise credit	1.7	1.7
Capital stock	0.1	0.1
Retained earnings[a]	(1.1)	(0.9)
Total net worth	(1.0)	(0.8)
Total	$ 6.8	$ 7.2

[a] The retained earnings are negative largely because of preinvestment expenses.
SOURCE: Company records.

employ 419 local workers, plus 14 expatriates during the
first year, and an average of 8 expatriates during the following 9 years.

The plant began operation in the last half of 1967 with parts
and components imported from factories owned by Michigan Motors in the United States, United Kingdom, and
Continental Europe. Company records show that sales and
profit through mid-1971 were approximately as shown in the
proposal, except for a drop in sales one year because of a
devaluation of the Asiana currency.

NET EFFECTS OF THE INVESTMENT

For all the case studies we prepared estimates showing how the foreign investment affected three important items in the U.S. economy: the U.S. balance of payments, the number of U.S. jobs, and the skill level of U.S. jobs.

The estimates for this case show that for the first two years the impact on the U.S. balance of payments was negative, but after that it was positive for all years. The recoupment period was 2.3 years. This is shown at a glance in Figure 2-1. (The dollar estimates for this and other such figures will be elaborated in tables later in the chapter, in this case Table 2-9.)

In contrast, the net impact on U.S. employment was positive in all years. Hence the recoupment period was

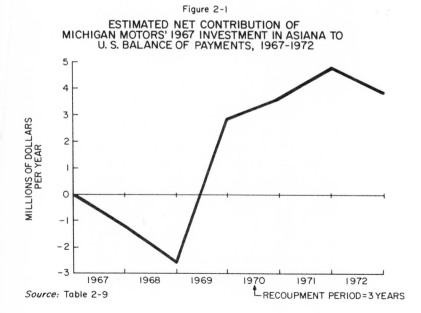

Figure 2-1

ESTIMATED NET CONTRIBUTION OF
MICHIGAN MOTORS' 1967 INVESTMENT IN ASIANA TO
U. S. BALANCE OF PAYMENTS, 1967-1972

Source: Table 2-9

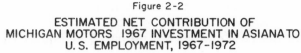

Figure 2-2

ESTIMATED NET CONTRIBUTION OF
MICHIGAN MOTORS 1967 INVESTMENT IN ASIANA TO
U. S. EMPLOYMENT, 1967-1972

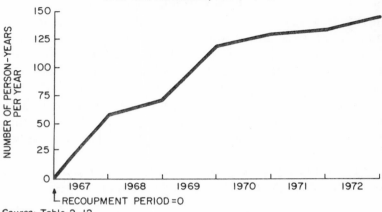

Source: Table 2-12

zero (Figure 2-2). Furthermore, these jobs added to the U.S. economy were on the average higher in skill levels than the average for all of U.S. manufacturing.

These conclusions were derived from two separate sets of estimates: (1) the U.S. balance of payments and employment *with* the 1967 investment in Asiana, and (2) the U.S. balance of payments and employment *without* the investment—on the assumption that no other U.S.-owned firm could expand outside the United States to serve the Asiana market. The second estimate (the "no investment" case) was then subtracted from the first (the "expansion" case) to obtain our estimates of the net effects of the investment in Asiana.

The estimates of the U.S. balance of payments and employment *with* the Asiana investment are relatively straightforward. These figures were derived primarily from the records of Michigan Motors, including their records of actual results of the project for the first few years and their projections for subsequent years. By far the more difficult set of projections concerned what would have happened *without* Michigan Motors' 1967 investment in Asiana. The critical question is, which manufacturers would have served the Asiana market and from what facilities?

What Would Have Happened Without the Investment?

One alternative that we quickly rejected is that any firm could export assembled vehicles to Asiana to serve the market that Michigan Motors lost due to the lackadaisical attitude of the local distributor. There are a sufficient number of non-U.S. automotive companies willing to assemble in Asiana to serve the local market so that, regardless of U.S. governmental policy, the Asiana market would be satisfied in accordance with the policies of Asiana, which call for local assembly. The growth of the automotive industries in the less-developed countries supports this conclusion: the number of vehicles manufactured and assembled in such countries increased from some 180,000 in 1955 to about 2,000,000 in 1969, and many of these vehicles were made by non-U.S. firms.[3]

We estimate that if Michigan Motors had not made its 1967 investment in Asiana, its market share would have continued to erode in line with the projections in the proposal submitted to the board of directors by the International Division. That is, the market share would have continued to drop for a while and then would have leveled

---

[3] For 1955 production and assembly, see U.N. Department of Economic and Social Affairs, *Statistical Yearbook, 1962* (New York: United Nations, 1963), pp. 264–265; for 1969 production and assembly, see U.N. Department of Economic and Social Affairs, *Statistical Yearbook, 1973* (New York: United Nations, 1974), pp. 309–311; also see annual reports of the auto companies.

out at about 12 percent. This seems plausible in view of the sharp drops in the market share of Michigan Motors in the two years prior to the investment, from 28 percent in 1964 down to 19 percent in 1965 and 15 percent in 1966. And two other factors support the conclusion.

First, the Asiana market seems to be highly competitive, judging by the variations in market shares from year to year of Michigan Motors and its main competitor, as shown in Table 2-2, and the rapid increase in the market share of Japanese companies (from 4 percent up to 28 percent within four years, as previously mentioned). It seems clear that sales are dependent on a good local operation.

Second, the members of our research team who prepared this case study found the actual results for the first several years of operations to be reasonably close to the estimates. This increased our confidence in the estimator's knowledge of the Asiana situation and in his other calculations of what would have happened to the market share of Michigan Motors if the investment had not been made.

The assumption in all of our cases is that the foreign output of the other U.S. firms could not be increased to compensate for the market share lost by Michigan Motors. Thus, we estimate that foreign-owned companies not only would have to make up the market share lost by Michigan Motors but also would have to provide capacity for all of the growth in Asiana's market. In accordance with industry practice we estimate market size in terms of number of vehicles, and we estimate the loss of Michigan Motors' share as slightly less than 4,000 vehicles a year and the growth of the Asiana market over the 1966 level as another 8,000 vehicles a year. Hence, if Michigan Motors had not invested, the total increase in foreign-owned assembly in Asiana would be some 12,000 vehicles a year, at least within a few years. This number is trivial by comparison with the capabilities of the non-U.S. firms in world automotive industry. For example, manufacturing plants in Japan, none of which were American-owned, exported 859,000 vehicles in 1969; and 183,000 of these, many of which were locally assembled, went to Asian countries.[4] Production of automotive vehicles outside the United States had been growing faster than that in the United States (Table 2-4), and by 1967 substantially exceeded that of the United States. Furthermore, much of this growth has been by non-U.S.-owned companies, for the U.S.-owned share of world output has declined, from 77 percent

TABLE 2-4

MOTOR VEHICLE PRODUCTION IN 1967 IN SIX LEADING COUNTRIES WITH LARGEST PRODUCTION, AND GROWTH RATE FROM 1957 TO 1967

	Production (millions of units)	*Percentage Increase 1957–1967*
United States	9.0	25
Japan	3.1	1,450
Germany	2.5	108
France	2.0	122
United Kingdom	1.9	72
Italy	1.5	275
Total, six largest producers	20.0	
Total, world	24.1	
Six largest producers as a percentage of world	83	

SOURCE: Automobile Manufacturers' Association, *International Trade and Investment* (Detroit, June 10, 1968).

[4] Society of Motor Manufacturers and Traders, Ltd., *The Motor Industry of Great Britain* (London, 1970), pp. 270–277.

in 1955 down to 45 percent in 1971. The share made *in* the United States declined even further, from 67 percent in 1955 down to 32 percent in 1971 (Table 2-5). This general pattern is consistent with the belief that foreign investments were necessary to prevent the Americans from losing an even greater share of the world market than they already had.

Thus it seems apparent that foreign companies would have no difficulty in providing all of the vehicles needed for the Asiana market.

But a more interesting question is whether the non-U.S. firms could have provided all of the *world's* growth in vehicle production if the U.S. firms had not been allowed to expand their output outside the United States. Again the answer seems apparent. *U.S.-owned* production outside the United States expanded from 3.9 million vehicles in 1965 to 4.2 million in 1971, an increase of some 300,000. By contrast, the foreign-owned firms increased their production by some 30 times this amount, from 9.3 million to 18.5 million, an increase of some 9.2 million; and all of their production was outside the United States. Thus, if U.S. firms had not expanded their foreign production at all, then the foreign firms would only have had to expand production by 9.5 million rather than 9.2 million. This would have required an annual growth rate of 12.5 percent rather than the 12.1 percent actually experienced, a seemingly easy task (Table 2-6).

Even if we had decided that John Adams' 12 percent estimate of Michigan Motors' eventual market share in Asiana was too low and had kept it at the 15 percent experienced in 1967, our conclusions would not have changed substantially. The recoupment period would still be reached during the third year (calculated by adjusting exports for the "no investment" case upward for 1968–1972 by 25 percent).

TABLE 2-5

WORLD MOTOR VEHICLE PRODUCTION BY U.S.-OWNED FIRMS, 1955–1971

	Millions of units			Percentage of total world production		
Year	In United States	In United States and Canada	In World	In United States	In United States and Canada	In World
1955	9.2	9.7	10.4	67	71	77
1956	6.9	7.4	8.2	59	63	70
1957	7.2	7.6	8.6	58	62	69
1958	5.1	5.5	6.7	45	49	59
1959	6.7	7.1	8.5	48	51	61
1960	7.9	8.3	10.0	48	50	61
1961	6.7	7.0	8.6	44	46	56
1962	8.2	8.7	10.5	46	48	58
1963	9.1	9.7	11.9	45	48	59
1964	9.3	10.0	13.1	42	46	60
1965	11.1	12.0	15.1	46	49	62
1966	10.4	11.3	14.4	42	45	58
1967	9.0	9.9	12.8	38	41	53
1968	10.9	12.0	15.2	38	42	54
1969	10.2	11.5	15.2	34	39	51
1970	8.3[a]	9.5	13.3	28	32	45
1971	10.7	12.0	14.9	32	36	45

[a] Strike reduced production.

SOURCE: Motor Vehicle Manufacturers Association of the United States, Inc., *1971 World Motor Vehicle Data* (Detroit, 1972), p. 4.

TABLE 2-6
ADDITIONAL GROWTH RATE REQUIRED OF FIRMS NOT U.S.-OWNED
TO SUPPLY VEHICLES TO ALL COUNTRIES OUTSIDE THE
UNITED STATES IF U.S.-OWNED FIRMS HAD NOT
INCREASED FOREIGN OUTPUT, 1965 TO 1971

	Millions of units		Annual growth rates 1971 over 1965
	1965	1971	
Actual production outside U.S.:			
By U.S.-owned firms	3.9	4.2	1.3
By non-U.S. firms	9.3	18.5	12.1
Total, outside U.S.	13.2	22.7	
Production outside U.S. if additional output of U.S.-owned firms had instead been supplied by non-U.S. firms:			
By U.S.-owned firms	3.9	3.9	0
By non-U.S. firms	9.3	18.8	12.5
Total, outside U.S.	13.2	22.7	

SOURCE: The Society of Motor Manufacturers and Traders Limited, *The Motor Industry of Great Britain, 1966* (London, 1966), pp. 25–29; The Society of Motor Manufacturers and Traders Limited, *The Motor Industry of Great Britain 1972* (London, 1972), pp. 29, 31–37; and annual reports of the U.S. auto companies.

Balance of Payments

Table 2-7 shows the flows that were recorded on the U.S. balance of payments through 1970 and our estimates for future years. During all years, merchandise exports, especially those of unassembled vehicles, caused the largest single flow, but the direct investment flows, chiefly in the form of loans and merchandise credit, also were important.

Table 2-8 shows that without the investment virtually all

TABLE 2-7

ITEMS ESTIMATED TO BE RECORDED ON U.S. BALANCE OF PAYMENTS
WITH MICHIGAN MOTORS' 1967 INVESTMENT IN ASIANA, 1967–1972
(millions of dollars)

Item	1967	1968	1969	1970	1971	1972
Merchandise Exports:						
Assembled vehicles	.4	.5	.6	.6	.6	.7
Unassembled vehicles	5.0	5.9	7.2	7.6	8.0	8.5
Equipment	.9	0	0	0	0	0
Service Exports:						
Dividends and interest	0	0	.4	.5	.5	.5
Management fees	.6	0	0	0	0	0
Direct Investment:						
Equity	0	.3	0	0	0	0
Loans from parent	−2.6	−1.4	1.3	1.3	1.3	.1
Loans from parent's credit corporation	0	−1.0	−1.0	−1.0	0	0
Merchandise credit	0	−1.4	−.7	−.3	−.2	−.2
Total	4.3	2.3	7.8	8.7	10.2	9.6

NOTES:

Merchandise Exports: Assembled vehicles—About 250 vehicles in 1967, rising gradually to 360 vehicles in 1972. (The numbers of vehicles are approximate to avoid disclosing confidential data.) SOURCE: Actuals for 1967–1970, company projections for other years.

Merchandise Exports: Unassembled vehicles—About 2,400 vehicles in 1967, rising gradually to 4,100 vehicles in 1972. (The numbers of vehicles are approximate to avoid disclosing confidential data.) SOURCE: See prior entry.

Merchandise Exports: Equipment—Company records. This sum is equivalent to 75 percent of the improvements in plant and equipment plus tooling needed for projected volumes of vehicles.

Service Exports: Dividends and interest—Flows from Asiana based on company records to mid-1971 and company projections beyond this. Flows from Europe estimated to be equal to average income receipts that U.S. automotive manufacturers received on European shipments in 1966. All income, including royalties and fees as well as dividends, was included here because of the small total.

(Continued on next page.)

TABLE 2-7 (*continued*)

SOURCE: U.S. Department of Commerce, *U.S. Direct Investment Abroad, 1966, Part 1: Balance of Payments* (Washington, D.C.: Superintendent of Documents, 1970).
Service Exports: Management fees—Preinvestment expenses.
Direct Investment: All accounts—Company records through mid-1971 and projections after this time.

TABLE 2-8
ITEMS ESTIMATED TO BE RECORDED ON U.S. BALANCE OF PAYMENTS
IF MICHIGAN MOTORS' 1967 INVESTMENT IN ASIANA
HAD *NOT* BEEN UNDERTAKEN, 1967–1972
(millions of dollars)

Item	1967	1968	1969	1970	1971	1972
Merchandise Exports:						
Assembled vehicles	.4	.3	.3	.3	.3	.3
Unassembled vehicles	5.0	4.6	4.6	4.7	5.0	5.3
Equipment	.1	0	0	0	0	0
Service Exports:						
Dividends and interest	0	0	.1	.1	.1	.1
Total	5.5	4.9	5.0	5.1	5.4	5.7

NOTES:
Merchandise Exports: Assembled vehicles—About 250 vehicles in 1967, dropping in 1968, and then rising very slightly through 1972. (The numbers of vehicles are approximate to avoid disclosing confidential data.) SOURCE: Our estimates are based on company projections of numbers of vehicles.
Merchandise Exports: Unassembled vehicles—About 2,400 vehicles in 1967, dropping in 1968, and then rising very slightly to 2,600 vehicles in 1972. (The numbers of vehicles are approximate to avoid disclosing confidential data.) SOURCE: See prior entry.
Merchandise Exports: Equipment—Tooling needed for projected volumes of vehicles.
Service Exports: Dividends and interest—Income receipts estimated to be received by U.S. parent because of European shipments to Asiana. SOURCE: See notes to Table 2-7.

of the balance-of-payments flows would have been from exports, primarily of unassembled vehicles.

We obtained the *net* effect of the investment, shown in Table 2-9, by subtracting the flows that we estimate would have existed without the investment from those existing with the investment (Table 2-8 subtracted from Table 2-7). During the first two years of the project the net effects are negative because of the large outflow of funds, primarily

TABLE 2-9

ESTIMATED *NET* CONTRIBUTION OF MICHIGAN MOTORS' 1967
INVESTMENT IN ASIANA TO U.S. BALANCE
OF PAYMENTS, 1967–1972

(millions of dollars)

Item	1967	1968	1969	1970[a]	1971	1972
Merchandise Exports:						
Assembled vehicles	0	.2	.3	.3	.3	.4
Unassembled vehicles	0	1.3	2.6	2.9	3.0	3.2
Equipment	.8	0	0	0	0	0
Service Exports:						
Dividends and interest	0	0	.3	.4	.4	.4
Management fees	.6	0	0	0	0	0
Direct Investment:						
Equity	0	− .3	0	0	0	0
Loans from parent	−2.6	− 1.4	1.3	1.3	1.3	.1
Loans from parent's credit corporation	0	−1.0	−1.0	−1.0	0	0
Merchandise credit	0	−1.4	−.7	− .3	− .2	− .2
Annual total	−1.2	−2.6	2.8	3.6	4.8	3.9
Cumulative	−1.2	−3.8	−1.0	2.6	7.4	11.3

[a] Balance-of-payments outflow is recovered in 1970; recoupment period is three years.

SOURCE: Table 2-8 subtracted from Table 2-7.

in the form of loans and merchandise credits. But after the first two years, the increased exports of vehicles more than offset the negative financial flows.

We did not consider the impact of certain other factors, such as the effect of Asiana's operations on the efficiency of Michigan Motors' operations elsewhere; but Asiana's operations are so small in comparison to Michigan Motors' worldwide manufacturing network that this effect would be minimal.

Number of U.S. Jobs

Table 2-10 shows the U.S. employment that we estimate existed as a result of the Michigan Motors' investment. Some 50 person-years of work were created during 1967 because of the export of equipment and 30 because of preinvestment work by U.S. corporate staff. But, from 1968 onward, the employment was virtually all due to the exports of the U.S. vehicles. The number of person-years of U.S. employment parallels the gradual rise in exports.

Table 2-11 shows the lower level of employment that we estimate would have occurred in 1968 because of the reduced exports that would have been experienced if Michigan Motors had not made the investment. Except for the person-years of work created in 1967 by the preinvestment analysis and exports of tooling, a certain amount of which was required regardless of who owned the facilities, the person-years all derive from exports of vehicles. The number of these person-years rises slowly from 1968 through 1972.

Table 2-12 shows our resulting estimate of the net contribution of the investment to U.S. employment levels. This net is positive in all years and shows a gradual increase as the difference in U.S. exports between the ''in-

TABLE 2-10
U.S. Employment Estimated to Exist as a Result of Michigan
Motors' 1967 Investment in Asiana, 1967–1972
(person-years)

Item	1967	1968	1969	1970	1971	1972
Merchandise Exports:						
Assembled vehicles	18	21	25	25	25	29
Unassembled vehicles	188	224	274	289	304	323
Equipment	50	0	0	0	0	0
Management Services	30	14	8	8	8	8
Total	286	259	307	322	337	360

Notes:

For rationale in defining entries, see Table 2-7.

Merchandise Exports: Assembled vehicles—Calculated by Harvard casewriters on the basis of 42 person-years per $1 million of exports; this includes employment in industries selling to automotive industry (SIC 371, motor vehicles and parts). Source: U.S. Bureau of the Census, *Census of Manufactures, 1967* (Washington, D.C.: Superintendent of Documents, 1971), Vol. 11, Industry Statistics, Part 3.

Merchandise Exports: Unassembled vehicles—Same as for assembled vehicles except four person-years per $1 million from estimate (obtained in industry interview) that about $100 of labor is needed to assemble one car; at $5 per hour, 2,000 hours per year, and $2,500 per vehicle, this gives $250,000 of vehicles per person-year.

Merchandise Exports: Equipment—Calculated by Harvard casewriters from industry averages in *Census of Manufactures.*

Management Services—Calculated by Harvard casewriters and author on assumption that preinvestment expenses spent in United States (Table 2-7) were for average of $20,000 per person-year.

vestment" and "no investment" cases continues to widen.

The reason U.S. net employment effects can be positive in all years whereas the balance-of-payments effects are negative the first two years is because we assume that the outflow of funds for the Asiana investment does not affect employment in the United States. This is in line with our assumption, discussed in Chapter 1, that the magnitude of

TABLE 2-11

U.S. EMPLOYMENT ESTIMATED TO EXIST IF MICHIGAN MOTORS
HAD *NOT* MADE ITS 1967 INVESTMENT IN ASIANA, 1967–1972

(person-years)

Item	1967	1968	1969	1970	1971	1972
Merchandise Exports:						
Assembled vehicles	18	13	13	13	13	13
Unassembled vehicles	188	175	175	179	190	201
Equipment	6	0	0	0	0	0
Management Services	15	0	0	0	0	0
Total	227	188	188	192	203	214

NOTES:
For rationale in defining entries, see Table 2-8.
Employment per unit is the same as for Table 2-10. The main difference in management services between this case and the "investment case" is that engineering design is omitted in the "no investment" case.

TABLE 2-12

ESTIMATED *NET* CONTRIBUTION OF MICHIGAN MOTORS' 1967
INVESTMENT IN ASIANA TO U.S. EMPLOYMENT, 1967–1972

(person-years)

Item	1967	1968	1969	1970	1971	1972
Merchandise Exports:						
Assembled vehicles	0	8	12	12	12	16
Unassembled vehicles	0	49	99	110	114	122
Equipment	44	0	0	0	0	0
Management Services	15	14	8	8	8	8
Annual Total	59	71	119	130	134	146
Cumulative	59	130	249	379	513	659

SOURCE: Table 2-11 subtracted from Table 2-12.

U.S. foreign direct investment flows is so small that the effects of such flows on the levels of U.S. investment and overall economic activity are offset by U.S. monetary and fiscal policy. Hence, in fact, the most important employment effect is the change in the skill level of jobs in the U.S. work force.

Skill Level of U.S. Jobs

We estimate that a total of 659 person-years of employment were created by the investment during the first six years of the project. Forty percent of these were high-skill jobs, a higher proportion than the 34 percent average for all U.S. manufacturing. This is primarily because the skill levels of the U.S. automotive industry and its suppliers are higher than the average; but it also results partially from the exports of equipment and the utilization of main office staff in the project study and operations. Table 2-13 shows the summary of the estimates.

* * * * *

This case is consistent with the best model yet developed to show the effects of U.S. foreign direct investment on the U.S. balance of payments (the Hufbauer-Adler model), since it illustrates that merchandise trade is more important than financial flows in determining the net balance-of-payments flows resulting from foreign direct investment.[5]

However, this case differs from the Hufbauer-Adler model in that the major competitors of the U.S. companies are not locally owned firms, but firms owned outside the host country.[6]

---

[5] Hufbauer and Adler, *Overseas Manufacturing Investments and the Balance of Payments* (Washington; U.S. Treasury Department, 1968), Chapter 5.

[6] Although Hufbauer and Adler recognize that the competitors of U.S. companies can be from third countries rather than from the host country (ibid., pp.

TABLE 2-13

NET EFFECT OF MICHIGAN MOTORS' 1967 INVESTMENT IN ASIANA ON U.S. SKILL LEVELS FOR FIRST SIX YEARS OF PROJECT COMPARED WITH AVERAGE OF ALL U.S. MANUFACTURING

	Mix of job skills (percent)	
	Created because of investment in Asiana	Average for U.S. manufacturing[a]
Professionals	16	15
Skilled	24	19
Clerical and sales	12	16
Semiskilled and unskilled	48	50
Total	100	100
Two highest skill levels[b]	40	34
Two lowest skill levels	60	66

[a] Bureau of Labor Statistics, U.S. Department of Labor, *Tomorrow's Manpower Needs,* Vol. IV, revised 1971, Bulletin 1737 (Washington, D.C.: U.S. Government Printing Office, 1972), pp. 33–35.
[b] Defined as "professionals" and "skilled."

5, 70), their model and some conclusions drawn therefrom assume that the competitors are from the host country (ibid., pp. 23, 26, 33, 46, 70, 71).

3

Serving the Market of a Developed Country: Tire Manufacture in Canada

IN EARLY 1969 THE EXECUTIVE COMMITTEE of a large U.S. tire company, described in this case under the disguised name of International Tire Company (Intertire), approved a request for $8.3 million from Intertire's wholly owned Canadian subsidiary to expand its existing tire-manufacturing plant in a town which we call by the disguised name of Josette, in Quebec, Canada. The proposal called for expanding the existing capacity from 4,000 to 6,000 tires per day.

The additional tires were needed for Intertire's anticipated sales increase in Canada. Not surprisingly, the alternative of not providing the tires to its potential customers was not considered. Since 1947 Intertire had maintained between 20 and 24 percent of the Canadian tire market (Table 3-1) and it was not about to let this business go to others by default. Furthermore, in line with the strategy of vertical integration followed by all major tire-manufacturing companies, Intertire did not consider the alternative of purchasing the tires from another company.

In 1921 Intertire had begun production of tires in Canada, in Ontario, to serve all of Canada; this plant was expanded several times. As the western market grew, Intertire opened its second Canadian factory in Alberta. In 1965 it opened a third plant—the one in Josette—to serve Quebec. Besides the usual tradeoffs between economies of scale and freight costs, a new factor encour-

TABLE 3-1

APPROXIMATE SHARE OF CANADIAN TIRE MARKET SERVED BY FIRMS WITH IMPORTANT POSITIONS IN CANADIAN MARKET, SELECTED YEARS, 1947–1969

(percent)

Manufacturer	1947	1951	1956	1964	1969
U.S. manufacturers:					
Intertire	20	23	19	21	24
U.S.—Firm A	11	14	10	10	9
U.S.—Firm B	37	34	30	34	35
U.S.—Firm C	18	16	19	19	18
Other U.S.	5	5	11	6	5
Subtotal, U.S.	91	92	89	90	91
Non-U.S.:[a]					
Dunlop (U.K.)	9	8	11	10	9
Total	100	100	100	100	100

[a] Sales of other non-U.S. firms, not exceeding 3 percent of the total market, are not included because of lack of data.

SOURCE: Estimated by authors from Dominion Bureau of Statistics, *Rubber Products Industry,* 1952, p. A-8, and interviews with a U.S. tire manufacturer other than Intertire.

aged Intertire to build the Josette plant: "economic nationalism" had taken a strong upswing in Quebec, and General Motors had announced that the tires for the vehicles to be made in a new GM plant in Quebec would be obtained from suppliers making the tires in Quebec. This was extremely important because tires for new vehicles, so-called "original-equipment" business, accounted for 35 percent of all tire sales in Canada; and the industry believed that the sale of replacement tires was heavily influenced by the original equipment.[1]

Although we did not obtain a complete record of the discussion that took place in Intertire's executive committee meeting, the decision to serve the Canadian market by expanding in Canada rather than in the United States was probably an easy one. Many years ago the American tire manufacturers, with the inducement of Canada's protective tariff, which at one time was as high as 22.5 percent, had concluded that making tires in Canada was desirable in order to have an important position in the Canadian market. The strategy seemed to work: U.S. tire manufacturers have captured some 90 percent of the Canadian tire market. By 1969 Canada's tariff had been reduced to 20.5 percent and was scheduled for a reduction to 17.5 percent in 1972, still a formidable barrier to overcome with U.S. production.

The growth in the Canadian market for tires had been given an important boost by the increased number of new cars built in Canada as a result of the Canadian-U.S. Automotive Agreement, which made most trade between Canada and the United States in vehicles and parts duty-free; but this did not include tires. The Automotive Agreement helped fuel Canadian economic growth, by

---

[1] Statistics are from the Rubber Association of Canada and the Dominion Bureau of Statistics.

facilitating the increase in Canadian exports of automotive products from $76 million in 1964 to $2.6 billion in 1968, or some 20 percent of all Canadian exports. In 1969, rises of 7.5 percent in Gross National Product and 8 percent in capital investment were expected.

Industry observers estimated that by 1969 Intertire had increased its total Canadian capacity to 20,850 tires per day, and its Canadian production was almost up to capacity.[2] Observers predicted a shortage of capacity for 1970 and the years beyond.

In 1969 Intertire management considered four possibilities for adding Canadian capacity:

(1) Increase Josette capacity by 50 percent (this proposal was the one eventually adopted);
(2) Again expand the much larger plant in Ontario;
(3) Construct a new plant in Ontario; and
(4) Construct a new plant in Nova Scotia in order to obtain a greater geographical spread.

Intertire did not make available to the Harvard researchers comparative cost figures for all alternatives, but management implied that Josette's efficiency and proximity to the large and growing market in Quebec were the primary factors influencing the decision to expand there. The executive committee approved the financial plans shown in Table 3-2.

As Table 3-2 indicates, the Intertire managers assumed that the plant would begin production at full capacity at the beginning of 1970 and operate at full capacity during the ensuing years, with no change in the price level. Further, they planned to obtain all of the funds for the expansion from Canada. The Canadian expansion did not

---

[2] Interview with company other than Intertire.

TABLE 3-2

FINANCIAL FLOWS: PROPOSAL FOR INTERTIRE'S 1969 EXPANSION
OF ITS JOSETTE PLANT, 1969-1975

(millions of Canadian dollars)

	1969	1970	1971	1972	1973	1974	1975
Capital appropriation	6.7	0	0	0	0	0	0
Working capital	0	1.6	0	0	0	0	0
Total investment	6.7	1.6	0	0	0	0	0
Net sales	0	9.3	9.3	9.3	9.3	9.3	9.3
Costs	0	7.5	7.4	7.4	7.4	7.4	7.4
Profit before tax	0	1.8	1.9	1.9	1.9	1.9	1.9
Taxes	0	1.0	1.0	1.0	1.0	1.0	1.0
Profit after tax	0	.8	.9	.9	.9	.9	.9
Depreciation	0	.4	.4	.4	.4	.4	.4
Cash flow	0	1.2	1.3	1.3	1.3	1.3	1.3
After-tax return on investment percent	0	10	10.5	10.8	10.8	10.8	10.8

PAYOUT: On basis of profit after tax = 9.4 years (figure appearing in appropriation request submitted to Intertire's Executive Committee).
On basis of cash flow = 6.4 years (figure calculated by Harvard case
researchers).

SOURCE: Company.records; except authors changed capital appropriation from
1970 to 1969, because it is unlikely that the new facilities operated at
full capacity during the year in which the capital was expended. Also, we
disguised certain figures above, and others in this chapter, which were
obtained from company records, in order to maintain confidentiality, but
not so as to change our quantitative or qualitative conclusions.

prevent Intertire from continuing to enlarge its operation
in the United States. The company spent well over $100
million for new U.S. facilities in 1969.[3]

---

[3] Estimated by authors from company's annual reports.

NET EFFECTS OF THE EXPANSION

As in our other cases, we prepared estimates showing how the 1969 expansion affected the U.S. balance of payments, the number of U.S. jobs, and the skill level of U.S. jobs.

The estimates show a slightly positive impact on the balance of payments during 1969, followed by a loss of some $6.5 million during 1970. However, a gradual improvement ensues, with the balance becoming slightly positive in the sixth year, reaching $1.46 million in the seventh year, and leveling off at this figure for each subsequent year (Figure 3-1).

Estimates of employment level follow a somewhat similar pattern—negative impacts of 100 and 183 person-years in the first and second years, respectively, gradually turn into a positive impact by the sixth year and stay positive during the succeeding years (Figure 3-2). This pattern results in a

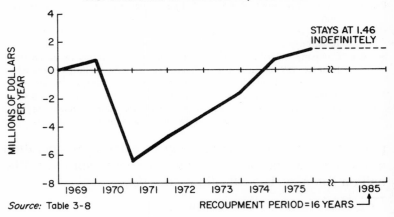

Figure 3-1

ESTIMATED NET CONTRIBUTION OF INTERTIRE'S 1969 EXPANSION IN CANADA TO U.S. BALANCE OF PAYMENTS, 1969-1985

Source: Table 3-8

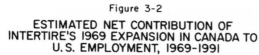

Figure 3-2

ESTIMATED NET CONTRIBUTION OF
INTERTIRE'S 1969 EXPANSION IN CANADA TO
U.S. EMPLOYMENT, 1969-1991

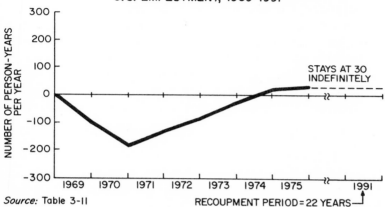

Source: Table 3-11 RECOUPMENT PERIOD = 22 YEARS

cumulative loss of 478 person-years of employment during the first seven years; these lost jobs are lower in skill levels than the average for all U.S. manufacturing or the average for the U.S. tire industry; on the other hand, the extra jobs that continue to exist indefinitely as a result of the Canadian expansion are higher in skill levels than jobs in U.S. manufacturing or in the U.S. tire industry.

As usual, we derived these conclusions from two sets of estimates: (1) the U.S. balance of payments and employment *with* the Canadian expansion, and (2) the U.S. balance of payments and employment *without* the Canadian expansion, assuming that no other U.S.-owned firm could expand outside the United States to serve the Canadian tire market. We then subtracted the second estimate, the "no expansion" case, from the first, the "expansion" case, to determine the effects of the Canadian expansion.

The estimates of the U.S. balance of payments and employment *with* the Canadian expansion are relatively straightforward. These figures, especially the balance-of-payments items, were derived mainly from the forecasts included in Intertire's appropriation request. But the critical estimates, for which we were forced to use a substantial amount of judgment, are the ones concerning what would have happened if the expansion had *not* occurred. By far the most important question to be answered is whether the tires for the expanding Canadian market would be made in the United States. To answer this question requires a knowledge of the competitive situation.

What Would Have Happened Without the Expansion?

The U.S.-owned companies not only dominated the Canadian market for tires—holding a market share of about 90 percent in 1969, as Table 3-1 shows—but owned about the same percentage of the production capacity in Canada.

In view of these dominant positions, we judge that Intertire—as well as other U.S. manufacturers—would have attempted to hold on to the Canadian market for some time even if expansion in Canada had been forbidden by the U.S. government. They would have exported from the United States and would have been willing to add capacity there in order to do so. Little risk would be involved, because later, when foreign competitors began to take over the Canadian market, the output from the U.S. facilities could serve the growth in the U.S. market.

As an alternative, Intertire could have made no attempt to serve any of the growth in Canada, letting the business immediately go to foreign firms. This choice would have been unlikely, because it would have produced a lower profit potential than attempting to serve the Canadian market by exporting from the United States.

Because of the large share that U.S. firms together had

in the Canadian tire market, it seems likely that these U.S. firms would have been successful in serving Canada from the United States, at least for a while. Canadian tire prices would have risen perhaps 10 percent to enable the U.S. firms to earn at least a modest profit on the U.S. exports.

But foreign competition would have been too strong to allow U.S. exports to capture the growth in the Canadian market for very long. To be sure, the U.S. tire companies did have larger sales worldwide than their major foreign competitors, the top three U.S. companies ranking 1, 2, and 4; but if the battleground is moved outside the United States, the picture changes—with the top three U.S. companies ranking 3, 4, and 6 in the world in 1971, for example (Table 3-3).

These foreign firms seem large enough to have the capability of capturing all of the growth in the Canadian market; collectively, they had a worldwide capacity of over 700,000 tires a day in 1969 (Table 3-4). Since some half of this capacity was outside the home countries, they seem to have had sufficient experience in operating facilities outside their own home country to manufacture in Canada if that became necessary. In addition, these firms had shown the ability to expand rapidly. For example, during the five years from 1964 to 1969, the three largest non-U.S. tire firms, Michelin, Dunlop, and Pirelli (the latter two merged in 1971), increased their production capacities by 190,000 tires per day worldwide, of which 112,000 was capacity of the investing firm outside the home country. These additions represent an annual growth rate worldwide of 13 percent and an annual growth rate outside the home countries of 16 percent.

If similar growth were experienced from 1969 to 1974, for instance, then the additional increase in their combined production capacity would be a large multiple of the ex-

TABLE 3-3

A Comparison of Sales of Major Tire Companies Worldwide Excluding United States
and Worldwide Including United States, 1971

Name	Nationality	Excluding United States (in billions of U.S. dollars)	Rank	Including United States (in billions of U.S. dollars)	Rank
Dunlop/Pirelli	U.K.-Italy	2.2[a]	1	2.4	3
Michelin	France	1.4[b]	2	1.5	5
Goodyear	United States	1.1	3	3.6	1
Firestone	United States	.7	4	2.5	2
Bridgestone	Japan	.5[c]	5	.5	8
Uniroyal	United States	.5	6	1.7	4
Continental	Germany	.4[c]	7	.4	9
Dunlop-Australia	Australia	.3[c]	8	.4	10
Goodrich	United States	.3	9	1.3	6
General	United States	Nil	10	1.0	7

[a] Based pro rata on number of factories and estimates of exports.

[b] On the assumption that $100 million of sales are in the United States.

[c] On the assumption that 90 percent of sales are outside the United States.

Source: Including U.S., from *Fortune* list of 500 largest U.S. firms and 300 largest foreign firms, *Fortune*, May and August, 1972. Excluding U.S., estimated by Dario Iacuelli and Jack Kirby; see Robert B. Stobaugh, et al., *The Likely Effects on the U.S. Economy of Eliminating Deferral of U.S. Income Tax on Foreign Earnings* (Cambridge, Mass.: Management Analysis Center, 745 Concord Avenue, 1973), p. 52.

TABLE 3-4
ESTIMATED CAPACITIES OF NON-U.S. TIRE MANUFACTURERS, 1964 AND 1969 [a]
(thousands of tires per day)

	Total	In home country	Outside home country
		1964	
Michelin	82	48	34
Dunlop	106	53	53
Pirelli	49	31	18
Subtotal	237	132	105
Other	134	N.A.	N.A.
GRAND TOTAL	371		
		1969	
Michelin	201	104	97
Dunlop	136	56	80
Pirelli	90	50	40
Subtotal	427	210	217
Other	282	N.A.	N.A.
GRAND TOTAL	709		
	Growth between 1964 and 1969		
Michelin	119	56	63
Dunlop	30	3	27
Pirelli	41	19	22
Subtotal	190	78	112
Other	148	N.A.	N.A.
GRAND TOTAL	338		

[a] These figures understate the size of non-U.S.-owned capacity, because if non-U.S. entities owned 50 percent or more of a factory, they were assumed to own only 50 percent; and if non-U.S. entities owned less than 50 percent, they were assumed to own no share in the factory. These assumptions, made because of lack of ownership details, could cause an error of no more than 10 percent.
SOURCE: Estimated by authors from data provided by company other than Intertire.

pected amount of U.S.-owned expansion in Canada, which between 1969 and 1974 was about 38,000 tires.[4] If these major foreign firms were to obtain all of the growth in the Canadian tire market, on the assumption that the Canadian sales of U.S. firms did not grow permanently over the 1969 levels, then their worldwide increase would have to be at an annual growth rate of 14 percent instead of 13 percent. Such a modest additional increase in production seems easily attainable by these firms.

In fact, the foreign firms could have been faced with handling an even larger expansion program. For if U.S. laws had been changed so that no U.S. tire company could have increased production in any country outside the United States, then the foreign manufacturers in order to prevent U.S. exports from capturing part of the growth in the foreign markets, would have had to make up a deficit worldwide, not just in Canada. But Dunlop, Pirelli, and Michelin would not have had to meet this challenge alone; other foreign firms also would have expanded. The growth rate in the tire capacity of the major foreign-owned tire firms—including others as well as Dunlop, Pirelli, and Michelin—was 14 percent annually from 1964 to 1969 despite U.S.-owned expansions.[5] This growth rate would have had to be stepped up to 18 percent annually from

---

[4] This assumes an 8 percent annual growth rate, which is the rate experienced in the Canadian replacement market from 1964 to 1968; this is lower than the 9 percent in the total market, but the latter includes the one-time boost in the original-equipment market caused by the Canadian-U.S. Automotive Agreement. On the other hand, the assumed growth rate of 8 percent is higher than the 5.5 percent annual growth rate experienced for all tire sales in Canada between 1956 and 1964, but this latter period does not reflect the higher speeds and resultant greater tire usage of the late 1960s. (SOURCES: calculated by authors from statistics of the Rubber Association of Canada and the Dominion Bureau of Statistics, and interview with company other than Intertire.)

[5] From 371,000 tires per day in 1964 to 709,000 tires per day in 1969 (Table 3-4), an increase of 91 percent, or 14 percent annually.

1969 to 1974.[6] In the absence of U.S.-owned expansions, this 18 percent growth rate seems within the capability of these foreign firms.

Foreign firms very likely would have the encouragement to expand in Canada of either or both the Canadian central government and a provincial government; for example, the Industrial Development Company of Nova Scotia invested 50 million Canadian dollars in the new Michelin plant to produce 12,000 to 20,000 tires per day; also, Michelin reportedly received the right of free entry into Canada of Michelin tires produced abroad.[7] And the foreign firms, until their Canadian plants began production, would have an advantage over U.S. tire companies in exporting to Canada. Their hourly labor costs are less than half those in the United States (Table 3-5), and this cost difference is believed not to be offset by differences in efficiencies between U.S. and foreign plants. Labor costs are about 20 percent of the total costs of making a tire in the United States.[8]

Any question about the ability of foreign producers to compete with U.S. exports in foreign markets should be dispelled by the growth of imports into the United States. In the face of the very strong distribution systems of the

---

[6] Projecting the growth of foreign-owned tire plants for another five years results in new capacity additions of 645,000 tires per day; adding this to the additional 196,000 tires needed outside Canada to make up the deficit caused by no U.S. expansions (calculated on the assumption that 1969 to 1974 growth is the same percentage as 1964 to 1969) and to the 38,000 tires needed in Canada results in a total expansion of 879,000 tires, an increment of 124 percent in five years, or 18 percent annually.

[7] "Dassault, Michelin Plan to Build Canadian Plants," *Wall Street Journal,* July 30, 1969, p. 14. D. E. Osborn and D. H. Thain, "The Michelin Tires Manufacturing Co. of Canada Ltd. (A)," (London, Ontario, Canada: University of Western Ontario, 1973), Case Number 3-374-815.

[8] U.S. Bureau of the Census, *Census of Manufactures, 1967* (Washington, D.C.: Superintendent of Documents, 1971), Vol. 11, Part 2, p. 30 A-11.

TABLE 3-5

ESTMATED HOURLY EMPLOYMENT COSTS OF TIRE-PRODUCTION
WORKERS IN MAJOR TIRE-PRODUCING COUNTRIES, 1970

(*in U.S. dollars, including fringe benefits*)

United States	6.00	United Kingdom	2.25
Canada	5.00	Italy	2.25
West Germany	2.85	Japan	1.75
France	2.35	Spain	1.05

SOURCE: Statement of the Rubber Manufacturers Association on November 25, 1970, to U.S. Tariff Commission.

U.S. manufacturers and the extra costs incurred because of freight and U.S. duties, U.S. imports of tires grew fivefold between 1963 and 1968, exceeding U.S. exports in 1967 and 1968, and reaching 6.5 percent of the U.S. domestic market in 1968.[9] The imports continued to grow, doubling between 1968 and 1971.[10]

We estimate that within six years—that is, by 1975—Intertire's U.S. exports of tires that would have been added if the Canadian plant had not been expanded would have dwindled to zero. This estimate, of course, is open to question.

For example, some might argue that the estimate of six years is much too long. The analysis above suggests that providing the necessary capacity to serve the Canadian market would not be a formidable task for the three major foreign producers—Dunlop, Pirelli, and Michelin. In addition, other possible sources exist, such as the Japanese. Both the European and the Japanese producers possess the required technology to serve the original-equipment and replacement sectors of the Canadian markets. They

[9] Statement of Rubber Manufacturers Association before the U.S. Tariff Commission, November 25, 1970.

[10] U.S. Department of Commerce, *U.S. Industrial Outlook, 1972* (Washington, D.C.: Superintendent of Documents, 1972), p. 182.

would have started with the original-equipment market, which is traditionally very price-sensitive, and would then have moved to the replacement market.

The entry of the non-U.S. firms would have been speeded if the original-equipment market were to switch to radial tires rather than the belted-bias tires normally used in the United States. As of 1970, foreign producers seemed to have definite advantages over U.S. companies in the production of radial tires; namely, their experience with product development, their more economical sources of steel wire, and their contacts with the suppliers of specialized equipment who had worked very closely with them. In case of a Canadian switch to radial tires, any attempt by U.S. producers to maintain a position in Canada would have required the U.S. producers and suppliers to invest hundreds of millions of dollars in a rapid switch-over to radials. Even then, American producers would still find themselves confronting at least equal and sometimes superior products priced substantially below their own because of the differential costs of labor, freight, and tariffs.

In addition, it is possible that the Canadian government would have insisted on a crash program of import substitution to reduce imports.

In contrast, others might argue that the estimate of six years is too short. Indeed there are important constraints on the rapid penetration of the Canadian market by non-U.S. producers:

(1) Labor strife, by causing production cutbacks and squeezing profits, was curtailing expansions in France and Italy in 1968–1970 and hence was reducing the capability of firms in these countries to export.[11]

---

[11] Henry Giniger, "Another Hectic Year Looms in France," *New York*

(2)   Except for the Japanese, most foreign production
was geared to the high-quality, high-price markets,
principally the market for radial tires. On the assumption that Canada would not switch to radials,
any attempt to penetrate the original-equipment
market would have required that foreign producers
develop and market a belted-bias tire for both the
original-equipment and the replacement markets;
and this would mean developing some new
techniques and installing new equipment. Alternatively, Canadian automakers, all of whom are
affiliates of the four U.S. automobile companies,
could have adapted their suspension designs to the
radial tire with a lag of perhaps two model years.
In this case, there would have been little penetration of the current nonradial replacement market
until some 18 months after the new model cars
rolled off the production line, that is, 3½ years
altogether.

(3)   U.S. automobile manufacturers required that
suppliers of original-equipment tires meet stringent
criteria on the number of dealerships, amount of
inventory, financial condition, and other characteristics. With the U.S. tire manufacturers in control of 90 percent of Canadian retail tire outlets, it
would have required several years for non-U.S.
firms to meet Detroit criteria.

(4)   Ties between the U.S.-owned Canadian automobile manufacturers and the U.S. tire companies were extremely close.

In addition to these constraints, it could be argued that
U.S. tire manufacturers might be willing to make no profit
and earn only a part of their normal 28 percent overhead

Times, January 16, 1970, p. 58; and Robert C. Doty, "Italy's Healthy Glow
Getting a Feverish Flush," *New York Times,* January 16, 1970, p. 66.

and thereby offset the 17.5 percent Canadian tariff and the Canadian wage differential, which is equivalent to another 2 percent of tire cost.[12] This pricing policy would help maintain their position in the Canadian market for original-equipment tires—an extremely important factor because of the common belief in the industry that the original-equipment market governs to a large extent the course of the replacement market. However, such action, by restricting construction of new facilities in Canada, might be ruled to be "dumping" and therefore might be prevented on the grounds that Canadian industry would be injured through U.S. firms' exporting to Canada at lower prices than those in the United States.

Although we think that a six-year transitional period represents a plausible estimate, others might reasonably estimate a transition period as short as three years or as long as nine years. But there is little doubt about the final outcome—Canadian plants would supplant the U.S. exports.

Armed with this six-year estimate, the researchers' task of estimating balance-of-payments and employment effects becomes relatively straightforward.

Balance of Payments

Table 3-6 shows the flows that we estimate to exist *with* Intertire's plant expansion in Canada. If the analysis stops here, it appears that the effects on the balance of payments are favorable in all years, for they are estimated as providing a surplus of $670,000 in the first year (1969) of the project, rising to $1.46 million annually during the third and each subsequent year. United States exports of merchandise dominate the statistics—$670,000 of equipment

---

[12] About a 10 percent wage differential on 20 percent of the tire cost.

TABLE 3-6

ITEMS ESTIMATED TO BE RECORDED ON U.S. BALANCE OF PAYMENTS
AS A RESULT OF INTERTIRE'S 1969 EXPANSION
IN CANADA, 1969–1975

(millions of dollars)

Item	1969	1970	1971	1972	1973	1974	1975
Merchandise Exports:							
Raw materials	0	1.22	1.22	1.22	1.22	1.22	1.22
Equipment	.67	0	0	0	0	0	0
Management Fees	0	.06	.06	.06	.06	.06	.06
Dividends	0	.16	.18	.18	.18	.18	.18
Total	.67	1.44	1.46	1.46	1.46	1.46	1.46

NOTES:

Merchandise Exports: Raw materials—The $1.22 million of annual exports of raw materials from the United States for the Canadian expansion were estimated to be split as follows: synthetic rubber, $1.12 million; textiles, $10,000; and other, $90,000. We calculated these figures by multiplying the cost of the tires by the percentage of the cost accounted for by each type of raw material obtained in the United States, as follows:

The cost structure for the expanded operation was approximately as follows (estimates of an Intertire manager):

Raw material		65.5%
Natural rubber	5.5%	
Synthetic rubber	19.0	
Reclaimed rubber	1.0	
Compounding chemicals	10.0	
Textiles	18.0	
Steel wire	1.0	
Others	11.0	
Labor		16.5
Overhead		18.0
Total		100.0%

We estimate the sources of these raw materials as follows (after discussion with Intertire managers):

TABLE 3-6 (*continued*)

	U.S.-based companies (including Intertire)	U.S. foreign affiliates (including Canada)	Canadian locals	World markets
Natural rubber	—	92.5%	—	7.5%
Synthetic rubber	80.0%	—	20.0%	—
Textiles	1.0	99.0	—	—
Others	5.0	—	95.0	—

Merchandise: Exports Equipment—We estimate that approximately 10 percent of the $6.7 million of fixed assets (plant and equipment) was imported from the United States (based on interview with Intertire manager).

Management Fees—An Intertire manager gave us the estimate that the parent, on an allocated basis, would render services at the rate of one person-year per one thousand tires of daily production in Canada; thus the Josette expansion requires two person-years each year. In addition, a further four person-years of home office work is allocated to Canada because of the increased sales that resulted from the expansion of Canadian capacity. These person-years, a composite of skill levels, are valued at $10,000 each or $60,000, or 0.6 percent of sales. (This fee is a substantially lower percentage of sales than the average of all U.S.-owned subsidiaries in the rubber-products industry in Canada, for which such fees averaged 1.4 percent of sales in 1966, the latest year for which such data are available; see U.S. Department of Commerce, *U.S. Direct Investments Abroad, 1966, Part I: Balance of Payments Data,* p. 162; and *Survey of Current Business,* October 1970, p. 20.)

Dividends—These are estimated by us, based on interviews with management, to be 20 percent of profits after taxes, which are assumed to be those shown in the proposal to the Intertire Executive Committee (Table 3-2). (This 20 percent compares with a 15 percent average for all U.S.-owned Canadian manufacturing subsidiaries in the rubber and miscellaneous plastics industry in 1966; *U.S. Direct Investments Abroad, Part I: Balance of Payments Data,* p. 172). No dividends are shown for profits on other Intertire foreign subsidiaries that provide natural rubber and textiles, for the amounts are negligible.

Certain items not appearing in the table merit comment:

Royalties—No royalties are charged. This is consistent with the practice of U.S.-owned subsidiaries in the rubber-products industry in Canada: *U.S. Direct Investments Abroad, Part I: Balance of Payments,* p. 156.

Imports of tires on automobiles—Approximately 1,500 of the additional 2,000 tires produced daily are sold to the Canadian original-equipment market. Some 5 percent of all original-equipment tires sold by Intertire in Canada are exported to the United States from Canada under the provisions of the Canadian-U.S. Automotive Agreement. However, because these exports from Canada to the

(*Continued on next page.*)

the first year (1969) and $1.22 million of raw materials in each succeeding year. Management fees and dividends were quite small by comparison, totaling only $60,000 plus $160,000, or $220,000 the second year, and $240,000 each subsequent year. Intertire's plans to obtain all funds in Canada result in no capital outflow from the United States. The notes with Table 3-6 provide further details for each estimate.

Table 3-7 shows the financial flows that we estimate would have existed if Intertire had *not* expanded its Canadian facilities. By far the most important figure is the U.S. exports of tires, which are estimated as $8.16 million in 1970. This is the price received by Intertire-U.S.; the Canadian customers would pay some $2 million in addition because of Canadian tariffs, freight, and handling in Canada, and profit for the Canadian subsidiary that sells the tires. These exports of tires would be supplemented slightly by dividends from Intertire-Canada's profits on the sales and offset slightly by U.S. imports of raw materials, with a resulting balance-of-payments surplus of $7.91 million in 1970, dwindling to zero in 1975.

In order to obtain a forecast of the net effects of the Canadian expansion on the U.S. balance of payments, the estimates of the U.S. balance of payments *without* the

United States would remain the same no matter where the tires were obtained, the author decided not to enter this flow on either the investment case or the hypothetical "no investment" case, since it does not affect the outcome of the analysis.

Direct investments abroad—All of the $8.3 million needed for the project was to be obtained in Canada and the principal and interest for the loan is paid from Canadian revenues, so the effect on U.S. capital flows is zero. Implicit in this estimate is the assumption that the use of funds in Canada does not cause any greater flow of funds from the United States into the Canadian capital and money markets than would exist if a non-U.S. firm had built the plant, nor does it reduce the flow of funds from Canada to the United States that might otherwise take place, e.g., an Intertire dividend.

TABLE 3-7

<small>ITEMS ESTIMATED TO BE RECORDED ON U.S. BALANCE OF PAYMENTS
IF INTERTIRE HAD *NOT* MADE ITS 1969 EXPANSION
IN CANADA, 1969–1975</small>
(millions of dollars)

Item	1969[a]	1970	1971	1972	1973	1974	1975
Merchandise Exports:							
Tires	0	8.16	6.40	4.80	3.20	.80	0
Dividends	0	.15	.12	.09	.06	.01	0
Merchandise Imports:							
Raw Materials	0	−.40	−.31	−.23	−.16	−.04	0
Total	0	7.91	6.21	4.66	3.10	.77	0

[a] The only item on the U.S. balance of payments that changed in 1969 as a result of the expansion was "exports of equipment," which were zero without the expansion. All other items are also shown as zero in 1969 without the expansion to be consistent with Table 3-6, which shows all items as zero except "exports of equipment."

NOTES:

Merchandise Exports: Tires—Estimates are placed at 2,000 tires per day in 1970, going to zero in 1975. A price rise of 10 percent to $10.2 million, over the expected price of sales, $9.3 million, from Josette was assumed in order to result in an estimated profit before taxes of 6 percent on sales, compared with the expected profit of 20 percent on sales if the Josette expansion had been made. Thus, in 1970, export sales from the United States would be valued at $10.2 million, with Intertire having a total cost of $9.58 million and profits before taxes of $.62 million.

The following is an approximate statement of costs and profits:

  Manufacturing costs (1.02 times Josette costs, on
  assumption that labor costs are only difference
  between United States and Canada. So cost difference
  would be about 10 percent of 20 percent, or 2 percent
  [wage differential from United States and Canadian
  government statistics rather than Table 3-5]) = 7.4
  (from Table 3-2) × 1.02 =   7.55
  Freight and handling in United States (assumed

(Continued on next page.)

to be 4 percent of manufacturing costs) =   .30
Profit to U.S. parent (about ½ of total profit) =   .31
   Transfer price to Canadian subsidiary =   8.16
   Canadian duty (17.5 percent of transfer price) =   1.43
   Freight and handling in Canada (assumed to be same
     as in United States) =   .30
Profit to Canadian subsidiary (about ½ of total
   profit) =   .31
Final sale price (set to give total profit to
   Intertire of 6 percent on sales, which results in a
   selling price 10 percent higher than from Josette) =   10.20

Thus, U.S. merchandise exports are $8.16 million, i.e., the transfer price.

The relationship of export sales value to final sales value is maintained throughout the five years in which it was assumed that tires would be exported from the United States. This assumed profit margin of 6 percent is our best judgment but has no support from empirical relationships. However, a substantial variation in this profit margin would have little effect on the conclusions.

Dividends—All of the after-tax profits on Canadian sales are assumed to be repatriated.

Merchandise Imports: Raw Materials—This is primarily natural rubber which would be imported into the United States for the tire production. The breakdown of raw materials and sources of raw materials is as shown in explanatory notes for Table 3-6.

Certain items not appearing on the table merit comment:

Exports of raw materials—This is now zero since the additional tires would not be manufactured in Canada; therefore the United States would export no additional raw materials. It is assumed that when foreign manufacturers commenced manufacture in Canada, they would obtain raw materials from their home countries because of their close relationships with their raw material suppliers. Synthetic rubber, which was the principal U.S. export of raw material for tires in Canada, is made by Intertire in the United States, but interviews with industry executives indicate that it is readily available outside the United States at competitive prices.

Exports of equipment—This is estimated to be zero, as the non-U.S. multinational enterprises—European and perhaps Japanese—would obtain their machinery from non-U.S. sources regardless of whether they attempted to serve the Canadian market by manufacturing in Canada or by exporting to Canada. Interviews with executives in the tire industry indicate that it is common practice in this industry for machinery manufacturers in the home country to work very closely with the tire producers, and, as a result, the tire-manufacturing equipment takes on somewhat of a proprietary nature.

expansion (Table 3-7) were subtracted from the estimates *with* the expansion (Table 3-6). The results are shown in Table 3-8.

The expansion, after having a slightly positive impact during the first year (1969), is estimated to have had a negative impact on the U.S. balance of payments of $6.47 million during the second year (1970), but to again become positive in the sixth year and leveling off at $1.46 million in the seventh year. By far the largest flow of funds is that connected with the export of tires that would have taken place from the United States to Canada if the Canadian expansion had not occurred.

In making these estimates, a number of factors are ignored because of the difficulty of quantifying them. For

TABLE 3-8

ESTIMATED *NET* CONTRIBUTION OF INTERTIRE'S 1969 EXPANSION IN CANADA TO U.S. BALANCE OF PAYMENTS, 1969–1975

(millions of dollars)

Item	1969	1970	1971	1972	1973	1974	1975
Merchandise Exports:							
Tires	0	−8.16	−6.40	−4.80	−3.20	−.80	0
Raw materials	0	1.22	1.22	1.22	1.22	1.22	1.22
Equipment	.67	0	0	0	0	0	0
Management Fees	0	.06	.06	.06	.06	.06	.06
Dividends	0	.01	.06	.09	.12	.17	.18
Merchandise Imports:							
Raw materials	0	.40	.31	.23	.16	.04	0
Annual total		.67	−6.47	−4.75	−3.20	−1.64	.69	1.46[a]
Cumulative		.67	−5.80	−10.55	−13.75	−15.39	−14.70	−13.24

[a] We assume that annual total remains at $1.46 million through at least 1985, when cumulative balance-of-payments outflow is recovered; recoupment period is 16 years.

SOURCE: Table 3-7 subtracted from Table 3-6.

example, what would have been the effect over the long run on the existing Intertire-owned facilities in Canada if Intertire could not expand? As non-U.S. firms expanded in Canada, it's very likely that they would become lower cost producers than Intertire because of economies of scale and might price their tires so that the profit margin on sales from the existing Intertire capacity would decline, thereby resulting in a decline in dividends and management fees. To the extent that this would happen, the effect on the U.S. balance of payments of expanding in Canada would be more positive than is shown in the analysis. Possibly offsetting this would be larger dividends during the first few years because funds would not be needed for expansion.

A second question is, would the United States continue to supply the raw materials to the Josette plant indefinitely? At some future time the raw materials might be manufactured locally, or Intertire might decide to obtain them from another country, in either case reducing the projected U.S. exports of $1.22 million in raw materials.

Third, would the close relations that would develop between foreign tire manufacturers and U.S. automakers in Canada result in a greater willingness on the part of U.S. automotive companies to import foreign tires into the United States?

Fourth, would some funds move from U.S. capital and money markets into Canadian capital and money markets in order to provide the funds raised in Canada for the Josette expansion?

Number of U.S. Jobs

We estimate that the Canadian expansion in Josette—looked at by itself and without consideration of alternative events—resulted in 22 person-years of work in the United

States in 1969, a figure that rose to 30 person-years in 1970 and stayed at that rate indefinitely. The 1969 employment is for the equipment manufacture; the subsequent employment represents mainly workers engaged in the manufacture of synthetic rubber, and personnel in the home office to provide services for Josette and to replace expatriates sent to Josette. Table 3-9 shows these estimates.

Yet, if the Josette expansion had not been undertaken, the additional employment in the United States would have been substantially greater during the early years—an estimated 122 person-years in 1969 for the manufacture of equipment required for the U.S. capacity expansion, and over 200 person-years in 1970 for the manufacture of tires for export to Canada and for Intertire management services. The person-years associated with both tire production and management services would decline to zero, parelleling the decline in the exports of tires. Table 3-10 shows these estimates.

Because tire capacity in the United States to serve the U.S. market also was being expanded, we assume that Intertire would not have excess capacity in the United States to manufacture the tires for the Canadian market. Further, we estimate that Intertire would have purchased equipment to provide this capacity, initially using it for the Canadian market but gradually shifting it to the production of tires for the United States. Thus, at first there would have been the creation of jobs for making and installing the equipment, but the allocation of this equipment to serve the U.S. market would make it unnecessary for Intertire to purchase an equivalent amount of equipment at that time. Therefore, less employment would be available during the years 1970 through 1975. Thus, the 122 jobs estimated to have been created in 1969 are lost during the ensuing five years.

TABLE 3-9

U.S. EMPLOYMENT ESTIMATED TO EXIST AS A RESULT OF
INTERTIRE'S 1969 EXPANSION IN CANADA, 1969–1975

(person-years)

Item	1969	1970	1971	1972	1973	1974	1975
Merchandise Exports:							
Raw materials	0	20	20	20	20	20	20
Equipment	22	0	0	0	0	0	0
Management Services	0	10	10	10	10	10	10
Total	22	30	30	30	30	30	30

NOTES:

Merchandise Exports: Raw Materials—The $1.2 million of raw material exports annually creates 20 person-years of employment as follows (from company records):

Item	Exports *(in millions of dollars)*	Employment *(person-years)*
Synthetic rubber	1.100	14
Textiles	.015	2
Compounding materials, chemical and misc.	.085	4
Total	1.200	20

Merchandise Exports: Equipment—Production of $670,000 worth of tire-manufacturing equipment in the United States created 22 person-years of employment. *U.S. Bureau of the Census, Census of Manufactures, 1967* (Washington, D.C.: Superintendent of Documents, 1971), Vol. 11, Industry Statistics, Part 3, p. 35 D-32.

Management Services—Two additional persons are required in the parent company to service Josette (calculated at the rate of one person per 1,000 tires per day); four additional persons in the parent company for general corporate overhead; and four persons in the United States operations to replace four additional expatriates needed at Josette.

Table 3-11 shows the net effects of Intertire's Canadian expansion on the level of U.S. employment. An initial negative impact of 100 person-years in 1969 rises to 183 in 1970 and then gradually turns into a positive impact, level-

TABLE 3-10

U.S. EMPLOYMENT ESTIMATED TO EXIST IF INTERTIRE HAD *NOT* MADE ITS 1969 EXPANSION IN CANADA, 1969–1975

(person-years)

Item	1969[a]	1970	1971	1972	1973	1974	1975
Merchandise Exports: Tires (including raw materials used in tires)	0	200	157	118	78	20	0
Management Services	0	40	28	21	14	4	0
Capital Expenditures in U.S.	122	−27	−23	−24	−35	−13	0
Total	122	213	162	115	57	11	0

[a] The only items for which we used a different level of employment in the United States as a result of the expansion were "exports of equipment" (Table 3-9) and "capital expenditures in United States" (Table 3-10). All items other than "capital expenditures in United States" are shown as zero in Table 3-10— "exports of equipment" were zero and all other items are shown as zero to be consistent with Table 3-10, which shows them as zero.

NOTES:

Merchandise Exports: Tires—Employment during 1970 would have been 200 person-years, declining thereafter as exports declined. Only part of this would have been within the tire industry, an estimated 132 person-years in 1970 for tire manufacture (calculated from actual plant data made available by a company other than Intertire). Employment to produce the raw materials made in the United States and used in the tires is estimated at 68 person-years in 1970, as follows:

Item	Value (in millions of dollars)	Employment (person-years)
Synthetic rubber	1.4	17
Textiles	1.3	32
Compounding materials, chemicals, and miscellaneous	.3	19
Total	3.0	68

Management Services—Five persons would have been needed only for the first year for the plant expansion; 35 persons would have been allocated to provide

(*Continued on next page.*)

ing off at 30 person-years in 1975. As with the balance of payments, the most important factor is tire exports.

The estimated net cumulative employment effect for the first seven years is a negative 478 person-years, as calculated from Table 3-11. Since the estimates for both the

TABLE 3-11

ESTIMATED *NET* CONTRIBUTION OF INTERTIRE'S 1969 EXPANSION IN CANADA TO U.S. EMPLOYMENT, 1970–1975

(person-years)

Item	1969	1970	1971	1972	1973	1974	1975
Merchandise Exports: Tires (including raw materials used in tires)	0	−200	−157	−118	−78	−20	0
Raw materials	0	20	20	20	20	20	20
Equipment	22	0	0	0	0	0	0
Direct Investment Fees and royalties: Management services	0	−30	−18	−11	−4	6	10
Capital Expenditures in U.S.	−122	27	23	24	35	13	0
Annual total	−100	−183	−132	−85	−27	19	30[a]
Cumulative	−100	−283	−415	−500	−527	−508	−478

[a] We assume that annual total remains at 30 person-years through at least 1991, when cumulative employment loss is recovered; recoupment period is 22 years.
SOURCE: Table 3-10 subtracted from Table 3-9.

services for the expanded plant. This latter number would have declined proportionately with exports, reaching zero in 1975.

Capital Expenditures in U.S.—We assume that an existing building would have been used but that $4 million would have been spent for capital equipment, thereby resulting in 122 person-years of employment in 1969. However, in later years as U.S. exports to Canada dropped, this equipment would have been used to manufacture tires for the U.S. market, thereby substituting for new U.S. equipment. We estimate that this substitution would have been 27 person-years in 1970. For 1971 through 1974 the employment figures are negative, representing the shifting each year of more U.S. capacity to serve the U.S. rather than the Canadian market.

"expansion" and "no expansion" cases showed positive employment effects, this number should be interpreted as meaning that an additional 478 person-years of employment would have been created in the United States during the years 1969 through 1975 if Intertire had not expanded in Canada; but as shown in Table 3-11, the expansion creates 30 person-years yearly beyond 1975.

Skill Level of U.S. Jobs

The 478 person-years not created during the years 1969 through 1975 as a result of Intertire's Canadian expansion—according to the estimates—contain a lower proportion of professional and skilled employees than the average for all U.S. manufacturing, 24 percent versus the 34 percent existing on the average in U.S. manufacturing (Table 3-12). This is because the jobs in tire

TABLE 3-12

NET EFFECT OF INTERTIRE'S 1969 CANADIAN EXPANSION ON U.S. SKILL LEVELS FOR FIRST SIX YEARS OF PROJECT COMPARED WITH AVERAGE OF ALL U.S. MANUFACTURING

	Mix of Job Skills (percent)	
	Not created because of Canadian expansion	Average for U.S. manufacturing[a]
Professionals	10	15
Skilled	14	19
Clerical and Sales	21	16
Semiskilled and Unskilled	55	50
Total	100	100
Two highest skill levels[b]	24	34
Two lowest skill levels	76	66

[a] Bureau of Labor Statistics, U.S. Department of Labor, *Tomorrow's Manpower Needs*, Vol. IV, revised 1971, Bulletin 1737 (Washington, D.C.: U.S. Government Printing Office, 1972), pp. 33–35.
[b] Defined as "professionals" and "skilled."

manufacture—the largest single block of U.S. jobs not created because of the Canadian expansion—are relatively low in skill levels. In contrast, the jobs created in the United States because of the Canadian expansion were relatively high skilled, being predominantly in equipment manufacture or in Intertire's main office.

In summary, the employment effects of Intertire's 1969 Canadian expansion were relatively large and negative in numbers for the first five years, and positive, but not so large, thereafter. The net effect on skill levels was to avoid the creation for five years of mostly low-skilled jobs in exchange for a relatively small number of high-skilled jobs lasting indefinitely.

*   *   *   *   *

This case is consistent with the best model developed to date to show the effects of U.S. foreign direct investment on the U.S. economy (the Hufbauer-Adler model) in that it illustrates the great importance of the merchandise trade flows as opposed to capital flows, management fees, and dividends.[13] However, this case reveals details not embodied in the Hufbauer-Adler model.

First, if Intertire had not invested abroad, foreign production would have substituted for U.S. exports gradually over a six-year period, whereas the Hufbauer-Adler models assume either immediate substitution or no substitution ever.[14]

---

[13] G. C. Hufbauer and F. M. Adler, *Overseas Manufacturing Investments and the Balance of Payments* (Washington, D.C.: U.S. Treasury Department, 1968).

[14] Ibid., pp. 33–47.

Second, this case shows the importance of existing communication links in affecting exports. For example, U.S.-owned tire plants in Canada likely would import more equipment and raw materials from the United States than non-U.S.-owned plants. In contrast, the Hufbauer-Adler model is based on an estimate that the propensity of all non-U.S.-owned firms in Canada to obtain capital equipment and raw materials in the United States is approximately the same as that of U.S. subsidiaries.[15] The Hufbauer-Adler estimates were obtained from regression models in which all manufacturing firms in Canada were assumed to be the competitors of all U.S.-owned manufacturing subsidiaries, rather than just foreign-owned firms being the competitors of the U.S. firms as in this case. Implicit in the use of these regression analyses is the lack of recognition that the principal competitors of U.S. multinational enterprises might be non-U.S.-owned multinational enterprises headquartered in Europe or Japan rather than Canadian firms.

Finally, this case is an example in which all funds for the expansion were obtained from outside the United States, an alternative not considered in the Hufbauer-Adler model.[16]

However, the main virtue of this case is to show the dilemma of the United States as a nation in facing a tradeoff between losing very large exports in the first year or two of the life of a foreign plant in exchange for longer run participation in the Canadian market, with its resulting U.S. exports of raw materials and U.S. receipts of income from the direct investment.

---

[15] Ibid., pp. 24, 28.

[16] Ibid., p. 14.

4

Using Low-Cost Resources for "Third-Country" Markets: Fruit Canning in Africa

IN 1969 A U.S.-BASED MULTINATIONAL ENTERPRISE, described in this case under the disguised name of American Food Processors (AFP), agreed to purchase an existing company engaged in growing and canning pineapple and other fruit in an East African country. The actual purchaser was AFP's subsidiary in the United Kingdom, which was to use the cannery as a source of supply in place of fruit previously purchased from unaffiliated companies in Africa. The cannery was being operated by the local government on a caretaker basis following bankruptcy of the previous owners in 1968.

This purchase was consistent with AFP's long-range strategy that had evolved through the years. AFP had developed a line of some 300 food products, many of which had originally been considered luxury items. But in time many of the luxury items began to take on the appearance of commodities; product quality became more standardized and price competition more severe. From AFP's viewpoint this evolution was both good and bad. It was good because of the accompanying enormous expansion of the market, first in the United States and then abroad. But it also facilitated the entry of independent canners into the business, especially outside the United States, where they produced at lower cost than canneries in the United States. AFP's counterstrategy was to build up its canning facilities abroad.

By 1970, as a result of this evolutionary process, AFP had some 20 food-processing plants in the United States, additional plants in 13 foreign countries, and licensing agreements with unaffiliated firms in a number of countries. Its foreign affiliates sold products in over a hundred nations, and foreign sales were between one-quarter and one-half of all sales of the enterprise.

Pineapple followed this general picture. Sometime during the 1960s AFP's wholly owned U.K. subsidiary, AFP-U.K., found that pineapple from the United States, mostly from Hawaii, was too expensive for the U.K. market. Thus, AFP-U.K. switched its source of supply from AFP-U.S. to Africa. But the result was not a perfectly satisfactory one, for the quality of the canned fruit obtained from Africa was not consistent over time. Though AFP was able to sell the African product in the United Kingdom, its inconsistent quality tended to detract from AFP's brand image as a supplier of high-quality products. So it is not surprising that the company, upon learning that an East African cannery was for sale, began to pursue the opportunity.

The initial discovery of the cannery came by accident—an AFP representative on a routine purchasing tour of East Africa in late 1968 stumbled onto it. He found that the firm, which had been the original owner of the facility, described in this case under the disguised name of East African Canners, Limited, had gone bankrupt in March 1968. It is difficult for outsiders, especially after the fact, to know exactly why; and insiders are reluctant to talk. But "poor management" was the reason commonly accepted by the local business community. The local government, having a vested interest in keeping the pineapple industry alive, formed a holding company to lease the assets from the liquidators and operate the plant until a purchaser could be found.

The facility consisted of both a factory and a ranch. The factory was quite complete. It included not only a main building with canning equipment but also a number of auxiliaries such as warehouses, boilers, workshops, an office building, and living quarters for European and local workers. Plant operations were tied closely to pineapple harvests and therefore were carried on only four months a year. During these four months, the plant sometimes operated as much as 20 hours a day.

The ranch, which provided about three-quarters of the pineapple needed by the cannery, consisted of both purchased and leased land. In addition to several buildings, it also had modern equipment such as tractors, trailers, and harvesters.

In January 1969, an AFP task force visited East Africa to evaluate the opportunity, including the technical, political, and economic aspects. Upon inspecting the facilities, the team decided that it would be desirable to change the layout of some existing equipment, purchase additional equipment, and build more warehouse space. The task force estimated that these changes and additions were necessary for the plant to produce at its nominal annual capacity of 20,000 tons of pineapple and 12,000 tons of other products. Further changes could be made later to increase capacity to 30,000 tons of pineapple and 18,000 tons of other products.

The task force investigated the local political and economic outlook by talking with a variety of people, both in East Africa and in the United Kingdom, including bankers, businessmen, university professors, lawyers, and suppliers, as well as local government ministers. The conclusions were quite favorable; the host country was judged to be very stable politically and to have an adequate labor supply at reasonable wages. AFP felt that if it gave technical assistance to East African farmers it could easily secure ample quantities of pineapple with the desired characteristics to maximize its yield. Estimates showed that a case of canned fruit from the East African facility could be delivered to the United Kingdom at a cost of $5.48 initially, and $5.26 after the yields had been improved and capacity operation achieved. (The mix of cases would include 62.5 percent pineapple and the remainder other fruit.) This compared with a price of $5.88 for current purchases from Africa and an incremental cost of $7.01 for fruit delivered from AFP's facilities in the United States (Table 4-1). And this last figure did not include fixed overhead.

After this trip, the big decision was almost a certainty. But a bargain had to be struck with the liquidators and the local government; funds had to be obtained, and the organization of AFP had to be modified to accept the new facility. As it turned out, these decisions were interrelated.

The negotiations had to satisfy several goals. The

TABLE 4-1

ESTIMATED COMPARATIVE COSTS[a] OF CASE[b] OF CANNED FRUIT FROM
FACILITIES OF AMERICAN FOOD PROCESSORS,
EAST AFRICA VERSUS UNITED STATES, 1970

(dollars per case, delivered to United Kingdom)

Item	East Africa[c]	United States	Savings, East Africa versus United States
Raw fruit	1.57	2.82	1.25
Sugar	.37	.35	−.02
Packaging	2.00	1.75	−.25
Labor	.33	.85	.52
Overhead	.31	.08[d]	−.23
Total FOB	4.58[c]	5.85	1.27
Freight	0.90	1.16	.26
Total CIF	5.48[c]	7.01	1.53[c]

[a] Excluding profit.

[b] A case of 24 No. 2½ cans, of which 62.5 percent is pineapple and the remainder other fruit.

[c] These costs are for the first year of AFP's operation of the facility; they were expected to be lowered by $.22 a case within several years through yield improvements and operation of the plant at capacity. This would result in a CIF cost of $5.26 and a saving of $1.75 over the U.S. product. These costs include an adjustment for the lower productivity experienced in Africa compared with the United States.

[d] Excludes fixed overhead.

SOURCE: Company records.

liquidators had one goal: money. The government had two goals: a successful commercial venture and a relatively minor involvement by the government. AFP had three goals: a profitable operation, high-quality product, and minimum risk, which AFP management equated with a minimum cash investment. These goals were congruent in that all parties wanted AFP to have the leading role and manage the operation, but there was one catch: no one wanted to invest much money. But given good management and a secure market, money is seldom an unsolvable problem. In this case a local agricultural development bank solved it by putting up $644,000, of which $625,000 was a long-term loan and $19,000 was for 10 percent of the equity. AFP put up $152,000 for 80 percent of the equity, and the local government $19,000 for the remaining 10 percent. With this capitalization of $815,000, the new company was able to obtain from two local banks overdraft credits totaling $610,000 for the first year, expandable to $1,500,000 in later years as needed.

Thus, the goals were met. The liquidators were paid for plant, inventories, and growing crops. The government owned only 10 percent of the equity but had confidence that AFP's commitment would insure a commercial success. And AFP, with an investment of only $152,000, owned 80 percent of the equity and had management control of an operation with total assets of over $1.5 million.

On the surface the project seems to have a relatively large portion of borrowed funds; by some standards, though, the balance sheet was a respectable one. The 1.6 ratio of current assets to current liabilities is larger than that of many U.S.-owned subsidiaries abroad;[1] and the ratio of paid-in capital to fixed assets almost met a rule of thumb sometimes used by U.S. multinational enterprises for their foreign subsidiaries—"let equity equal fixed assets."[2] The pro-forma balance sheet for the end of the first year (1970) is shown in Table 4-2.

The inclusion of the development bank affected the placement of the new company within the AFP family, because this bank, with its strong ties to Britain, looked

---

[1] See Sidney M. Robbins and Robert B. Stobaugh, *Money in the Multinational Enterprise* (New York: Basic Books, 1973), p. 128.

[2] Ibid., p. 57.

TABLE 4-2
PRO-FORMA BALANCE SHEET OF AFP'S EAST AFRICAN SUBSIDIARY,
1970–1974
(millions of dollars)

	1970	1971	1972	1973	1974
Assets					
Current	1.22	1.43	1.82	2.35	2.40
Growing crops	.13	.17	.21	.21	.21
Fixed (net)	.22	.20	.19	.24	.21
Total	1.57	1.80	2.22	2.80	2.82
Liabilities and equity					
Bank overdraft	.61	.83	1.14	1.57	1.47
Accounts payable	.15	.17	.24	.30	.30
Current	.76	1.00	1.38	1.87	1.77
Long-term loan	.62	.56	.50	.44	.38
Paid-in capital	.19	.19	.19	.19	.19
Retained earnings	0	.05	.15	.30	.48
Total capitalization	.81	.80	.84	.93	1.05
Total	1.57	1.80	2.22	2.80	2.82

SOURCE: Company records.

more favorably upon a venture with a U.K. firm than a U.S. firm. AFP decided to make AFP-U.K. the parent of the East African subsidiary.

Other factors supported this decision: the United Kingdom was to be the only market at first, and the other markets that might be served subsequently, such as other African countries and Continental Europe, were tied in more closely with U.K. operations than with U.S. operations. Furthermore, AFP-U.K. had sufficient depth in management to provide the expatriate managers that would be needed in East Africa. Finally, the earnings of the East African venture, by increasing AFP-U.K.'s profits by two percentage points, would be an important step for AFP-U.K. in its efforts to meet the goal of its "profit growth plan." This goal was a 12 percent return on equity in 1975.

The negotiations were conducted under pressure because of the deterioration of the plant and crops in the uncertain atmosphere of a caretaker management. A number of other ownership alternatives, ranging all the way from AFP's having a management contract with no ownership, to AFP's having a 90 percent ownership, were considered but were discarded. None met the objectives of the various parties as well as the 80-10-10 ownership finally agreed upon.

AFP began operation of the facility at the beginning of 1970. Table 4-3 shows the pro-forma income statement for the first five years of the project. After a year of break-even operation, the project shows a steady gain in profits as sales increase. Further, the cost of goods, per unit of output, improves slightly in the second and third years as the cost of produce declines because of yield improvements. Extraordinary expenses of $130,000 are required during 1970 and 1971 to improve the yield and increase capacity. Some $63,000 of the retained earnings is required for capital to finance capacity increases to make possible the sales growth shown in 1973 and 1974, for which time a production level of 30,000 tons of pineapple and 18,000 tons of fruit was planned.

Dividends of $80,000 yearly, equal to about 40 percent of paid-in capital, were to be distributed commencing in 1972. Table 4-2 shows the resulting pro-forma balance sheet.

NET EFFECTS OF THE INVESTMENT

We estimate that AFP's East African investment had a negative effect of $130,000 on the U.S. balance of payments in 1970, but a positive effect in all other years. The positive

TABLE 4-3

PRO-FORMA INCOME STATEMENT OF AFP'S EAST AFRICAN
SUBSIDIARY, 1970–1974

(millions of dollars)

	1970	1971	1972	1973	1974
Net Sales[a]	1.01	2.11	2.81	3.74	4.14
Cost of goods sold	−.95	−1.87	−2.46	−3.30	−3.64
Extraordinary expenses connected with improving yield and increasing capacity	−.02	−.11	0	0	0
Profit before taxes, R&D expenses, and royalties	.04	.13	.35	.44	.50
R&D expenses paid to AFP-U.K.	−.02	−.02	−.02	−.03	−.03
Royalties paid to AFP-U.K.	−.02	−.04	−.06	−.07	−.08
Profit before taxes	0	.07	.27	.34	.39
Local taxes at 33.3 percent	0	−.02	−.09	−.11	−.13
Profit after local taxes	0	.05	.18	.23	.26
Dividends	0	0	−.08	−.08	−.08
Retained earnings	0	.05	.10	.15	.18

[a] FOB, East Africa; the equivalent of 202,000 cases, each containing 24 cans of No. 2½ size, at $4.98 a case, for 1970. Price stays constant and quantities increase in subsequent years. Pineapple is 62.5 percent of total; other fruit is remaining 37.5 percent.
SOURCE: Company records.

effect starts at $30,000 in 1971 and climbs gradually to $80,000 by 1974, as shown in Figure 4-1. Sometime after 1974, when the local bank overdraft is reduced, the positive effect on the U.S. balance of payments increases further as dividends from the U.K. subsidiary increase, owing to larger dividends from the African subsidiary.

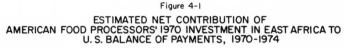

Figure 4-1

ESTIMATED NET CONTRIBUTION OF
AMERICAN FOOD PROCESSORS' 1970 INVESTMENT IN EAST AFRICA TO
U. S. BALANCE OF PAYMENTS, 1970-1974

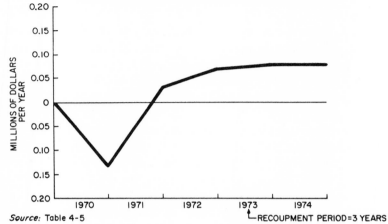

Source: Table 4-5   └─RECOUPMENT PERIOD=3 YEARS

We estimate that no employment effects in the United States would result from the East African investment.

These conclusions were derived by comparing estimates of actual occurrences with what would have occurred if the investment had not been made.

Estimates of actual occurrences are relatively straight-forward. The balance-of-payments flows were calculated from records made available by AFP (as summarized in Table 4-3). We estimated the employment effects at zero after discussing AFP's plans with AFP management. AFP had no plans to purchase equipment in the United States, and AFP-U.K. was to supply all expatriates needed by the East African subsidiary. True, some U.S. personnel investigated the East African investment opportunity, but this nominal amount of person-months is ignored.

What Would Have Happened Without the Investment?

To make an estimate of what would have occurred if AFP had *not* made the East African investment, the Harvard researchers used both AFP records and the published data on world production and trade in canned pineapple and processed fruits. We estimate that if AFP had not purchased the East African facilities, then AFP-U.K. would have continued to purchase canned fruit from Africa. Thus, U.S. exports of canned fruit would not have been affected.

The facts support this conclusion. As stated earlier, cost considerations had impelled AFP-U.K. to stop importing canned fruit from the United States some years before and to buy from Africa. Some cost comparisons were given in Table 4-1. In addition, data on world trade and production of pineapple show the loss of competitiveness of the United States compared with foreign producers.

For example, the U.S. share of U.K. imports of canned pineapple dropped from 6 percent in the 1963–1964 marketing season to 2 percent in the 1969–1970 season.[3] And during the same period the U.S. net trade deficit in canned pineapple grew from 4 to 22 percent of U.S. consumption because of a rise in U.S. imports and a fall in U.S. exports.[4] Further, U.S. production as a percent of world production dropped from 55 in 1961 to 45 in 1969.[5]

[3] *The Almanac of the Canning, Freezing, Preserving Industries* (Westminster, Maryland: Edward E. Judge and Son, 1971), p. 458.

[4] As a percentage of U.S. consumption, U.S. imports increased from 18 to 29 while U.S. exports declined from 14 to 7, expressed in terms of No. 2½ cans. *The Almanac of Canning, Freezing, Preserving Industries* (Westminster, Maryland: Edward E. Judge and Son, 1971), p. 458. U.S. Department of Agriculture, Economic Research Service, *Fruit Situation* (Washington, D.C.: U.S. Government Printing Office, 1971), July 1971, Table 10 and U.S. Department of Agriculture, Economic Research Service, *Fruit Situation* (Washington, D.C.: U.S. Government Printing Office, 1965), July 1965, Table 6.

[5] *The Almanac of Canning, Freezing, Preserving Industries*, p. 463.

The United States was losing its competitive advantage not only in pineapple but in processed fruits as a whole. In 1963, U.S. exports were 217 percent of U.S. imports; by 1969 the figure was 127 percent.[6]

It is doubtful that this growth in the competitive strength of foreign countries was caused by the establishment of U.S. plants abroad. Though market data are not available for canned fruit, data on the entire food industry show that foreign food companies are on the average larger than U.S. food companies, when considering either worldwide sales including the United States or worldwide sales excluding the United States (Table 4-4).

We estimate that if the $152,000 investment had not been made in Africa, the AFP-U.K. would have paid it in dividends to the U.S. parent. This assumes that if AFP had not allowed its British subsidiary to invest in Africa it would not have allowed it to invest in any other country, and thus AFP-U.K. would have been forced to return the funds to the United States. This dividend flow is the only balance-of-payments entry that would have resulted if the investment had not been made.

With the African investment, AFP-U.K.'s profits probably increase because it is able to obtain better quality fruit at the same price as it paid for prior purchases. However, AFP ignored this potential profit in its financial analysis. So did we.

Balance of Payments

Table 4-5 shows the net effects of the East African investment on the U.S. balance of payments. These are the estimates from which the simple chart, Figure 4-1, was derived. All effects are attributable to dividend flows. The

[6] U.S. Department of Agriculture, *1970 Handbook of Agricultural Charts* (Washington, D.C.: Superintendent of Documents, 1971), pp. 135–136.

TABLE 4-4
A COMPARISON OF WORLDWIDE SALES OF MAJOR FOOD COMPANIES,
BOTH EXCLUDING AND INCLUDING U.S. SALES, 1971

		Excluding U.S. Sales		Including U.S. Sales	
Name	*Nationality*	*U.S. (in billions of dollars)*	*Rank*	*U.S. (in billions of dollars)*	*Rank*
Unilever	U.K.-Neth.	6.4	1	7.5	1
Nestle	Switzerland	2.4	2	3.5	2
British-Am. Tobacco	U.K.	1.7	3	2.3	6
Assoc. British Foods	U.K.	1.5	4	1.5	10
Swift	U.S.	.4	5	3.0	3
Kraftco	U.S.	.4	6	3.0	4
General Foods	U.S.	.3	7	2.3	5
Beatrice	U.S.	.3	8	1.8	9
Armour	U.S.	.3	9	2.3	7
Borden	U.S.	.3	10	2.1	8

SOURCE: Including U.S., from *Fortune* list of 500 largest U.S. industrial firms and 300 largest foreign industrial firms, *Fortune* May and August, 1972; excluding U.S. estimated by Dario Iacuelli and Jack Kirby; see Robert B. Stobaugh, et al., *The Likely Effects on the U.S. Economy of Eliminating the Deferral of U.S. Income Tax on Foreign Earnings* (Cambridge, Mass.: Management Analysis Center, 745 Concord Avenue, 1973), p. 50.

investment results in $20,000 of dividends in 1970, climbing to $80,000 in 1974. These figures are based on the parent's intention that AFP-U.K., after paying appropriate U.K. taxes, would pay all dividends, research and development fees, and royalties received from Africa to the United States. The dividends growing out of the investment compare with the $152,000 ($.15 million) of dividends in 1970 if the investment had not been made.

TABLE 4-5

ESTIMATED EFFECTS OF AMERICAN FOOD PROCESSORS' 1970
INVESTMENT IN EAST AFRICA ON U.S.
BALANCE OF PAYMENTS, 1970–1974

(millions of dollars)

Item	1970	1971	1972	1973[c]	1974
With investment[a]	.02	.03	.07	.08	.08
Without investment[b]	.15	0	0	0	0
Annual difference = net annual effect of investment	−.13	.03	.07	.08	.08
Cumulative	−.13	−.10	−.03	.05	.13

[a] Calculated on the assumption that AFP-U.K. pays a 50 percent tax rate on dividends, R&D expenses, and royalties received from East Africa; receives a tax credit for the 33.3 percent tax paid in East Africa; and pays all remaining cash to the U.S. parent. (This is not exactly in accordance with all of the details of the tax laws of the United Kingdom or the United States, but is assumed for ease of exposition. This assumption has no important effect on the conclusions.) Thus, the U.S. parent would receive fees and dividends derived as follows:

	1970	1971	1972	1973	1974
R&D and royalties: paid to AFP-U.K.	.04	.06	.08	.10	.11
Received by U.S. parent	.02	.03	.04	.05	.05
Dividends: received by AFP-U.K. after paying a 16.7 percent income tax (50–33.3) on its 80 percent share of dividends	0	0	.05	.05	.05
Received by U.S. parent[d]	0	0	.03	.03	.03
Total received by U.S. parent	.02	.03	.07	.08	.08

Eventually, as the bank overdraft began to be reduced, dividends from East Africa might be increased.

[b] Calculated on the assumption that if AFP-U.K. had not invested the $152,000 in East Africa (for 80 percent of the equity), then it would have paid the $152,000 in dividends to the U.S. parent during 1970.

[c] Balance-of-payments outflow is recovered in 1973; recoupment period is three years.

[d] Rounding of the original data results in $0.3 million received by the U.S. parent from the dividends received by AFP-U.K. (rounded to $0.5 million).

Employment

No table of net employment effects is presented, because direct employment effects are estimated to be zero with or without the East African facility. Of course, there are indirect effects on both employment and the balance of payments, resulting from the income paid to the United States. But in accordance with the methodology used for all cases in this study, these indirect effects are not estimated. Rather, it is assumed that such income streams are either offset or greatly overshadowed by U.S. monetary and fiscal policy.

* * * * *

This case differs from the Hufbauer-Adler model showing how the U.S. balance of payments is affected by U.S. foreign direct investment in manufacturing in that U.S. merchandise trade flows are not altered by the East African transaction.[7] Instead, this case is consistent with some of the earlier views of foreign direct investment in which such investment was considered only in terms of financial flows.[8] However, the returns are substantially higher than the ones derived from the Hufbauer-Adler model or the earlier financial models, which typically showed recoupment periods in excess of seven years, and in some cases an infinite period, depending upon the assumptions.[9] In this case the recoupment period was less than three years. This shortness resulted in part because of the high financial leverage—88 percent of the funds were obtained from outside the enterprise's system compared with an average of 50 percent or so for U.S.-owned manufacturing facilities abroad.[10]

---

[7] G. C. Hufbauer and F. M. Adler, *Overseas Manufacturing Investments and the Balance of Payments* (Washington, D.C.: U.S. Treasury Department, 1968), Chapter 5.

[8] For example, see Philip Bell's model, described in ibid., p. 4.

[9] Ibid., pp. 4, 67, 68.

[10] Ibid., p. 16.

The view of AFP management was quite different from that of economists in judging balance-of-payments effects. This was a strategic investment to secure a satisfactory source of canned pineapple for its U.K. market and to offer the possibility of expanding into the European Economic Community and other countries. The financial flows were of secondary importance, for AFP's financial goal of minimizing its investment was achieved by putting up only $152,000 in order to obtain a source of supply of canned fruit that was expected to rise in value to $4 million annually by 1974.

Our pineapple story reveals one thing not embodied in any of the models to date—the role of U.S.-owned subsidiaries in owning and operating their foreign direct investments. In this case the U.K. economy is predicted to benefit from tax revenues and the increased employment opportunities for the home office personnel within AFP-U.K.

The case is consistent with studies showing that the U.S. industries which are most competitive worldwide are the ones paying relatively high wages,[11] for fruit-canning establishments in the United States pay lower wages than the average for all U.S. manufacturing—$4,826 yearly compared to $6,100 in 1967.[12]

[11] Helen Waehrer, "Wage Rates, Labor Skills, and United States Foreign Investment," in Peter B. Kenen and Roger Lawrence (*eds.*), *The Open Economy* (New York: Columbia University Press, 1968), pp. 19–39; and Irving Kravis, "Wages and Foreign Trade," *Review of Economics and Statistics*, XXXVIII (February 1956), pp. 14–30.

[12] For fruit-canning establishments, see U.S. Bureau of the Census, *Census of Manufactures, 1967* (Washington, D.C.: Superintendent of Documents, 1971), Vol. II, Industry Statistics, Part 1, p. 20C–38. For U.S. average, see U.S. Bureau of the Census, *Census of Manufactures, 1967* (Washington, D.C.: Superintendent of Documents, 1971), Vol. 1, Summary and Subject Statistics, p. 26.

5

Using Low-Cost Resources for the U.S. Market: Electronics Assembly in Taiwan

. . . multi-national firms can and do juggle the production of components and assembly operations to achieve maximum use of low-wage labor, using modern U.S. technology and operating at or close to U.S. productivity levels.[1]

No matter how efficient American producers and workers might be, they simply cannot compete in a labor-intensive industry such as consumer electronics with these extremely low wage rates and production based on U.S. techniques.[2]

LESS THAN 10 PERCENT OF THE OUTPUT of U.S.-owned plants overseas is exported to the United States,[3] but

[1] "International Trade," Report of the Economic Policy Committee to the AFL-CIO Executive Council, February 1970, p. 14.

[2] Floyd Smith, president of the AFL-CIO International Association of Machinists, quoted in the *Fort Lauderdale News and Sun-Sentinel*, February 8, 1970, p. 5H.

[3] U.S. Department of Commerce, *Special Survey of U.S. Multinational Enterprises, 1970*, November 1972, p. 23.

critics of U.S. multinational enterprises have put their spotlight on these plants when contending that U.S. investment abroad causes exports of American jobs; and in no industry has the impact been greater than in consumer electronics.[4] The charge has a strong political impact.[5] The products from the foreign plant are remarkably visible, and the mercantilist argument that a nation's market should be preserved for a nation's factories still has a strong emotional appeal.[6] Furthermore, the type of work moved abroad requires relatively low skills, so unskilled workers often are laid off in the United States; and it is difficult for proponents of U.S. foreign direct investment to answer the question: "What's going to happen to 50-year-old, uneducated workers laid off in Memphis?"[7] Although the U.S. workers in this question were not in Memphis, the case is the story of an investment made abroad to manufacture electronic items for the U.S. market.

The board of directors of Systek (a disguised name) in

[4] One of the early steps taken by the U.S. government to respond to the political pressure from unions was the study by the U.S. Tariff Commission on Item 807 of the U.S. Tariff Code, which provides that when U.S. components are sent to a foreign country and assembled into a product, the product may be imported into the United States and be subject only to duty on the "value added" by foreign labor, see John N. Kessler, "Item 807: A Boom . . . or a Bust for Electronics?" *Electronic Design,* April 26, 1970, pp. 24–26.

[5] The U.S. Treasury Department in 1973 proposed that such plants bear a tax penalty compared with other U.S. investments abroad. See Department of the Treasury, *Proposals for Tax Change,* April 30, 1973.

[6] Congresswoman Martha Griffiths stated that she was "horrified" to see that her Hoover sweeper was made in England; see *Hearings* on *In the Matter of Taxation of Foreign Income,* Ways and Means Committee, U.S. House of Representatives, February 28, 1973, p. 1,857.

[7] This question was being discussed by a number of people in Washington during the U.S. Tariff Commission Hearings concerning imports of television receivers in October 1971, about an RCA plant closed in Memphis, Tennessee. However, the announcement of the closing attributes it to a "lag in TV sales"; see *New York Times,* December 10, 1970, pp. 73–75.

late 1968 approved an investment of $1.9 million in equity for the establishment of a subsidiary in Taiwan to assemble automotive radios and certain automotive-radio components. The entire output of the plant was to be exported to Systek-U.S. and would substitute directly for work being done in a Systek factory in the United States.

The story starts in 1967, when two streams of events intersected, causing the Taiwan investment to be considered. After that, there was only a routine shepherding of a project through a corporate bureaucracy.

One stream of events concerned Systek's international business strategy. Systek, with domestic operations consisting of six major product groups containing over 40 operating divisions, had operated abroad for many years through its international division. This division, called Systek International, had its own president. It exported technologically sophisticated products, such as avionics equipment and controls; manufactured abroad less sophisticated products, such as brake shoes, primarily for local markets; and licensed a variety of items for manufacture by unaffiliated foreign companies. This mixture of wholly owned subsidiaries, joint ventures, and licenses was typical of U.S. firms with a broad line of relatively high technology products.[8]

The growth of international business had tripled in the previous ten years, though without the benefit of strong plans or policies. This situation changed in 1967 when Systek hired from outside the company a new president for Systek International. He immediately set about to adopt explicit long-range plans with stated policies on such matters as ownership preference. Especially relevant to the Taiwan project was the new executive's global view of

---

[8] John Stopford and Louis T. Wells, Jr., *Managing the Multinational Enterprise* (New York: Basic Books, 1972), p. 123.

trade and investment patterns. Based on his formal training in economics and his government experience in negotiating trade agreements, he had a firm conviction that as tariffs were lowered, many U.S. factories producing labor-intensive products would have more and more difficulty in competing with imports from low-wage areas such as Asia.

But the head of the international division, even if he had the backing of the president of the parent company, would have difficulty in forcing a foreign investment decision on one of the domestic operating divisions. So, in 1967, his suggestion at a corporate planning meeting that a domestic division should explore the possibility of low-cost manufacture in foreign locations seemed to make little impression on the group. To Systek executives in charge of domestic operations this was a novel idea which had never been discussed at such a planning meeting before.

The new executive, having failed to create any interest on his first attempt, tried a different tack—he cloaked the competitors as bogeymen and trotted them out to scare the domestic divisions. He wrote a letter to the heads of the domestic major product groups referring to the growing number of U.S. companies which had set up operations in foreign locations with low-cost labor, and he followed this up with conversations with executives of the domestic divisions.

Very likely these efforts would have been to no avail if another stream of events had not been flowing through one of Systek's domains—the "original-equipment" market for automotive radios served by Systek's Consumer Electronics Division (CED). Systek's solid business in this market, 85 percent of which was sales to U.S. manufacturers of cars, tractors, and mobile homes, and the remainder to U.S. dealers for installation in foreign cars, had begun to come under fierce attack.

The gradual standardization of designs and increases in competition had inevitably caused price to be considered the most significant factor in selling to automotive manufacturers. It was possible that one firm could command a small price premium because of a reputation for quality and reliability and for meeting contract performance, or because of an innovation in product design and engineering; but by 1967 Systek believed that the quoted prices of the major competitors were within 50 cents of one another, a small sum compared with the factory prices, which ranged from $17 to $70.

By late 1967 the competitive squeeze began to hurt. A U.S. manufacturer had offered to provide from its Japanese affiliates radios for Volkswagens at a lower price than Systek, and Mitsubishi proceeded to give an even lower quote. The result was that Systek sold its AM radios for foreign cars at an average price of $24 a unit, and made a profit of only 4 percent on sales, compared with prior profits of 10 percent or more. The squeeze was even greater on tractor radios; Systek was losing $4.49 on each unit (the unit price was $28).

Since even lower prices were projected for the future, CED management had been galvanized into an awareness of the problem and had begun groping for a solution. But CED managers did not have an answer. Further automation of the first stage in the process—the assembly of printed circuit boards (PCBs)—did not seem desirable because of the cost of the assembly machines and the difficulty of keeping them operating. And engineers felt that automation was not feasible for the second stage in the process—the assembly of PCBs and other components into a finished radio chassis. They held the same views about the third and final stage, that is, testing, assembling the chassis into a housing, packing, and shipping. Furthermore, the engineers doubted that extensive savings could be achieved by redesigning products. CED management had begun to perceive a glimpse of light: the plant would have to be moved from its high-cost location in the North, possibly to the southern part of the United States. At this critical moment, CED management received the proposal to consider moving part of its manufacturing operations overseas.

Given this merging of the two streams of events, the rest was routine. The building of a "commitment" began.[9] After several discussions with the international division, CED management decided that the possibility of foreign manufacture was worth investigating. To be sure, they were worried about the risks involved and the problems of setting up and controlling a plant overseas. But they thought that the possible cost savings might make offshore manufacture desirable for some of their products, particularly the simplest and most standardized items. The wheels were then in motion.

In early 1968 a Systek International division executive, who had lived in the Far East, visited several Far Eastern countries and, not surprisingly, reported that conditions appeared suitable for an investment in that area. He noted that wage rates were on the order of $20 per month for unskilled labor and emphasized the favorable experiences of other U.S. companies in manufacturing there. The head of the international division then sent a team to Taiwan, South Korea, and Hong Kong to investigate opportunities for the

---

[9] For discussions of this concept, see Yair Aharoni, *The Foreign Investment Decision Process* (Boston: Division of Research, Harvard Business School, 1966), pp. 122–141, 273–303; and Joseph L. Bower, *Managing the Resource Allocation Process* (Boston: Division of Research, Harvard Business School, 1970), pp. 68–69.

assembly of PCBs and auto radios. After a detailed study of government investment incentives, labor availability and quality, political conditions, the experience of other U.S. firms, and other factors, this team presented a report proposing that Systek establish a manufacturing plant in Taiwan.

The international division prepared a formal proposal with the aid of market forecasts by the Consumer Electronics Division. The proposal, which called for a fixed investment of some $2.5 million plus working capital, was accepted by Systek's board of directors in late 1968.

Some significant features of Systek's planned Taiwan investment were:

(1) Systek International would own 100 percent of Systek-Taiwan. The manager of Systek-Taiwan would report to both CED and Systek International.

(2) The Taiwan plant would make two types of printed circuit boards (PCBs) and two whole radio assemblies, called chassis—one AM model for tractors and one AM model for foreign automobiles. Systek-Taiwan would ship all products to CED, which would then use the PCBs to make additional whole radio assemblies, test and assemble all radio chassis into housings, and pack and ship all finished products.

(3) Initially, Systek-Taiwan would assemble components obtained from CED, but later would attempt to purchase components from suppliers in the Far East.

(4) The total number of employees in the Taiwan plant would increase to one thousand over a five-year period. About 80 percent would be unskilled workers, whom Systek-Taiwan would quickly train.

(5) Systek-Taiwan would purchase virtually all the equipment in the United States. Very few tools would be provided per worker for the assembly process; a pair of hand pliers usually would be sufficient.

(6) Most of the total fixed investment of about $2.5 million

would be financed by a Systek equity investment of $1.9 million in the Taiwan subsidiary. Requests for working capital were expected to rise over a five-year period to about $5.7 million. An initial $4 million loan from the parent company would be paid off over a three-year period, after which all working capital would be financed in Taiwan.

(7) Components shipped from Systek-U.S. to Systek-Taiwan would be invoiced at cost plus 10 percent. Except for 1969, when Systek-Taiwan would break even, the products shipped from Systek-Taiwan to Systek-U.S. would be priced to yield Systek-Taiwan a profit of 25 percent on the equity of $1.9 million, or 2.25 percent of sales, whichever was greater. Systek International and CED agreed on this pricing policy in order to provide what they considered to be a reasonable profit for Systek-Taiwan, but with the bulk of the overall Systek profit going to CED in order to encourage them to enter into the agreement. As with many goods traded between members of a multinational enterprise, there were no arm's-length transactions from which to derive a price.

Table 5-1 shows the pro-forma income statement for Systek-Taiwan. Profits stay at $480,000 yearly, or 25 percent of equity through 1972, and then begin to rise as 2.25 percent of sales exceeds $480,000. Table 5-2 shows Systek-Taiwan's pro-forma balance sheet. The seemingly low ratio (0.96) of current assets to current liabilities during 1969 results because the $4 million Systek-U.S. loan to Systek-Taiwan is shown as a current liability. As this intercompany loan is paid off, the ratio climbs to 1.35 in 1974—not unusually low for U.S.-owned subsidiaries abroad.[10] The policy of paying out half of earnings as dividends results in the total equity staying constant at about one-third of total assets.

---

[10] Sidney M. Robbins and Robert B. Stobaugh, *Money in the Multinational Enterprise* (New York: Basic Books, 1973), p. 128.

TABLE 5-1

PRO-FORMA INCOME STATEMENT OF SYSTEK'S
1969 TAIWAN INVESTMENT, 1969–1974

(millions of U.S. dollars)

	1969 (4 mos.)	1970	1971	1972	1973	1974
Net sales [a]	2.93	13.96	17.10	19.87	22.02	24.29
Costs [b]	2.93	13.48	16.62	19.39	21.52	23.75
Profits before taxes [a]	0	.48	.48	.48	.50	.54
Local income taxes [c]	0	0	0	0	0	0
Profits after taxes	0	.48	.48	.48	.50	.54
Dividends	0	.24	.24	.24	.25	.27
Retained earnings	0	.24	.24	.24	.25	.27
U.S. tax on dividends	0	.12	.12	.12	.12	.13
Dividends received by parent	0	.12	.12	.12	.13	.14

[a] The sales prices to Systek-U.S. were set to give Systek-Taiwan a profit of 25 percent on the equity investment of $1.9 million, or 2.25 percent on sales, whichever was greater. The controlling factor was return on equity in 1970, 1971, 1972, and return on sales for all years after 1972.

[b] For those readers interested in more details, following are estimated costs for 1970 and 1974.

	1970		1974	
	millions of dollars	*percent*	*millions of dollars*	*percent*
Direct labor	.118	0.9	.316	1.3
Burden	.674	5.0	1.050	4.4
Material	10.535	78.1	18.920	79.7
Shipping and duty	1.530	11.4	2.740	11.5
General and admin.	.620	4.6	.720	3.1
Total	13.477	100.0	23.746	100.0

[c] Local income taxes would commence after 1974.

SOURCE: Company records.

TABLE 5-2
PRO-FORMA BALANCE SHEET OF SYSTEK'S 1969 TAIWAN INVESTMENT,
YEAR ENDING SEPTEMBER 30, 1969–1974
(millions of U.S. dollars)

	1969	1970	1971	1972	1973	1974
Assets						
Current	3.25	4.91	6.03	6.95	7.68	8.48
Fixed	2.03	1.82	1.61	1.40	1.19	.98
Other	.24	.20	.16	.12	.08	0
Total assets	5.52	6.93	7.80	8.57	8.95	9.46
Liabilities and Equity						
Accounts payable for imports [a]	3.18	4.29	4.87	5.35	5.44	5.88
Local accounts payable and other current liabilities	.19	.25	.30	.35	.39	.42
Total current	3.37	4.54	5.17	5.70	5.83	6.30
Reserves and duty payable [b]	.25	.25	.25	.25	.25	.02
Paid-in capital	1.90	1.90	1.90	1.90	1.90	1.90
Retained earnings	0	.24	.48	.72	.97	1.24
Total equity	1.90	2.14	2.38	2.62	2.87	3.14
Total liabilities and equity	5.52	6.93	7.80	8.57	8.95	9.46

[a] Initially a parent-company loan; but after three years, monthly bank loans obtained through special "usance" credit scheme under which the Taiwan government makes available foreign exchange for plants that export their output.
  [b] Some $230,000 of this $250,000 is for duty payable on machinery and equipment. This duty does not become due until 1974.

SOURCE: Company records.

But the projected profits of Systek-Taiwan tell only a partial story, for it was planned that CED would get most of the benefits. Table 5-3 shows that CED's profits after taxes were projected to rise from $0.2 million during the

TABLE 5-3

PRO-FORMA STATEMENT SHOWING PROFITS OF SYSTEK'S CONSUMER
ELECTRONICS DIVISION ATTRIBUTABLE TO SYSTEK-TAIWAN'S
OPERATIONS, FISCAL YEARS, 1969–1974
(millions of U.S. dollars)

Product	1969	1970[a]	1971	1972	1973	1974[a]
Printed circuit boards for AM radios	.21	1.00	1.19	1.36	1.60	1.68
Printed circuit baords for AM/FM radios	0	.08	.20	.31	.35	.49
AM radios for foreign cars	.18	.60	.47	.24	.29	.31
Radios for tractors	.01	.11	.24	.25	.35	.42
Total profit before taxes	.40	1.79	2.10	2.16	2.59	2.90
Total profit after taxes[b]	.20	.90	1.05	1.08	1.30	1.45

[a] For those readers interested in more detail, profits before taxes as a percent of sales were estimated to be:

	1970	1974
PCBs for AM radio	21	23
PCBs for FM/AM radio	2	8
AM radios for foreign cars	9	3
Radios for tractors	11	10

[b] Taxes assumed to be 50 percent for ease in calculation.
SOURCE: Derived from company records.

truncated 1969 fiscal year to $0.9 million in 1970 and $1.49 million in 1974. A major share of these profits was expected to be from additional sales that CED would achieve because of the low-cost products from the Taiwan plant.

Thus, on a consolidated basis, the project looked very profitable. On its equity investment of $1.9 million and its three-year loan of $4 million, Systek's expected consolidated profits after taxes were $1.26 million in 1970, the first full year of operations, rising to $1.86 million in 1974 (Table 5-4). As nice as those projections were, they were secondary to what seemed to be the main purposes of the investment in Taiwan: survive at a profitable level in the automotive radio business, which was CED's apparent objective, and gain experience in manufacturing in low-wage countries for export, which was Systek International's apparent objective.

In the third quarter of 1969 the plant in Taiwan commenced operations and the first shipment of products was sent to CED shortly thereafter. During the fourth quarter of 1969, Taiwan production in terms of quantity and quality approximated that which had been included in the proposal approved by Systek's board of directors. The plant appeared to be a success.

But even if something starts well and ends well, the road

TABLE 5-4

PRO-FORMA STATEMENT OF SYSTEK'S CONSOLIDATED PROFITS AFTER
TAXES ATTRIBUTABLE TO ITS 1969 TAIWAN INVESTMENT,
FISCAL YEARS, 1969–1974

(millions of U.S. dollars)

Source	1969 (4 mos.)	1970	1971	1972	1973	1974
Earnings reinvested in Taiwan	0	.24	.24	.24	.25	.27
Dividends received by parent	0	.12	.12	.12	.13	.14
Additional earnings of Consumer Electronics Division	.20	.90	1.05	1.08	1.30	1.45
Total	.20	1.26	1.41	1.44	1.68	1.86

SOURCES: Tables 5-1 and 5-3.

along the way can be quite rocky, and such was the case of Systek-Taiwan. As operations proceeded in 1970, the outlook for the Taiwan operation began to appear less rosy. CED's U.S. market for automobile radios contracted as a decline in economic activity reduced demand for new automobiles. Those major car manufacturers that owned U.S. subsidiaries which supplied part of the manufacturers' radios drastically reduced their purchases from Systek in order to keep their own subsidiaries operating. CED, in turn, cut down on orders to the Taiwan plant and reneged on its bargain of letting transfer prices from Taiwan cover all costs plus at least a 25 percent return on equity. The way the books were kept, CED found that although reducing orders to Taiwan hurt Systek-Taiwan's profits, it boosted CED profits, since maintaining the employment level in the U.S. plant enabled CED to cover its large fixed overhead costs. CED continued to reduce its orders to Taiwan, so the Taiwanese results for 1970, shown in Table 5-5, were not as favorable as indicated in the original plan. In early 1971, CED ceased purchasing any items from the Taiwan plant. Soon afterwards CED moved its entire U.S. production of auto radios to a location in southern United States, where labor costs were approximately 70 cents per hour less than in the North.

The international division headquarters in New York sought business elsewhere for the Taiwan operation, but attracting new business takes time, so the Taiwan facility was shut down. Systek laid off the production workers but kept the managers and supervisors on the job. The wait was not long. By quoting very low prices, Systek managed to obtain orders from Canada and Europe, and so placed the facility back in operation. As of August 1971, the latest date for which information was available when the Harvard researchers had access to Systek data, the

TABLE 5-5
INCOME STATEMENT OF SYSTEK-TAIWAN,
PLANNED VERSUS ACTUAL, FISCAL 1970
(millions of U.S. dollars)

	Planned		Actual	
Net Sales		13.96		8.38
Direct labor	.12		.08	
Burden	.67		.48	
Material	10.54		6.14	
Shipping and duty	1.53		.94	
General and administration	.62		.43	
Costs		13.48		8.07
Profits before taxes and royalties		.48		.31
Royalty to parent[a]		0		.10
Local income taxes		0		0
Profits after taxes		.48		.21

[a] Paid after negotiations with U.S. Internal Revenue Service and Taiwan government.
SOURCE: Company records.

Taiwan facility was producing goods for Canada and Europe, but not for CED. The prices required to obtain the Canadian and European business were so low that Systek would have lost money if it had provided the products from its U.S. operations. Thus, in fact, these sales represented incremental business not available to the U.S. operations. International division management did not have firm estimates of future volume, but expected that the plant would be used to manufacture automotive radios for CED sometime in the future as well as products for other Systek operations in the United States and other parts of the world.

The turn of events in this case produced a dilemma for us, for there were now four alternatives that could be studied in two different analyses. The analysis of the first set of two alternatives would assume that the U.S. recession did not occur; in this analysis, what Systek expected to happen when they made the investment decision would be compared with what we estimate would have happened if the investment had not been made.

The second set of two alternatives would assume that the actual events of 1970 and 1971, including the recession and Taiwanese shutdown, did occur; in this analysis, what actually happened during the time for which we have data (the first year and a half of plant operations) and what we expected to happen subsequently would be compared with what we estimate would have happened if the plant had not been built.

We present the first two alternatives, that is, the analysis based on Systek's plans, for two reasons, one pragmatic and one theoretical.

The pragmatic reason is that we do not have sufficient data available to extend the analyses of the actual events past mid-1971. Our research contact in Systek, who was in the international division, said that his division had no projections for Systek-Taiwan and no information about subsequent automotive radio sales of CED, nor any knowledge of whether CED stopped making any products. The Taiwan plant had become a very sensitive subject and even the mention of it produced forlorn expressions on the faces of our acquaintances in Systek International. The warm welcome that we received in 1969 when we first wrote Systek-Taiwan as a teaching case had turned to embarrassed reticence at any reference to Taiwan. Since we do not have sufficient data available to make plausible projections without Systek's data on their CED operations, we abandoned this analytical path in favor of the other one.

The theoretical reason takes the following argument.

Because our goal is to determine the effects of decisions made to invest abroad, an analysis based on the environment predicted by the company when the investment decision was made is likely to be more representative than an analysis based on a set of events largely dominated by a U.S. recession. In other words, it can be argued that the environmental conditions assumed with the planned results are more representative than the recession which actually occurred. Hence, an analysis based on these environmental conditions likely applies to "normal" times and a decision under these conditions would be duplicated by many decision makers in other years. By contrast, an analysis using the first year and a half of Systek-Taiwan's operations would apply only to a plant built just prior to a recession which management did not expect to occur, and in fact which would not have been built if management had foreseen the economic downturn.

However, for those readers who are interested, an analysis of the first year and a half of the subsidiary's operations is provided in a postscript to this chapter. We believe that the major result of the recession was to delay the events predicted in the first analysis by several years.

NET EFFECTS OF THE INVESTMENT

Our estimates show that the Taiwanese investment initially caused negative effects on the U.S. balance of payments and employment; but within three years of plant start-up, the net annual effects are positive, as Figures 5-1 and 5-2 indicate. Furthermore, the cumulative net effects are positive for the balance of payments after four years and total employment after five years. The average skill levels of this net cumulated employment are higher than the averages of those existing in the electronics industry or in all the U.S.

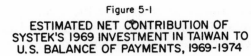

Figure 5-1

**ESTIMATED NET CONTRIBUTION OF
SYSTEK'S 1969 INVESTMENT IN TAIWAN TO
U.S. BALANCE OF PAYMENTS, 1969-1974**

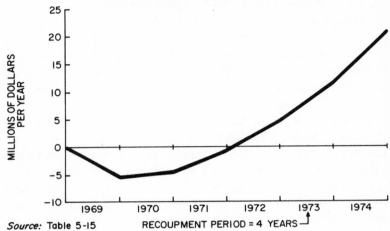

Source: Table 5-15   RECOUPMENT PERIOD = 4 YEARS

Figure 5-2

**ESTIMATED NET CONTRIBUTION OF
SYSTEK'S 1969 INVESTMENT IN TAIWAN TO
U.S. EMPLOYMENT, 1969-1974**

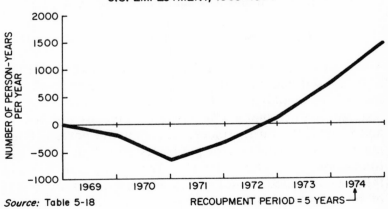

Source: Table 5-18   RECOUPMENT PERIOD = 5 YEARS

manufacturing industries. These net effects, of course, were obtained by subtracting our estimates of balance of payments and employment *without* the Taiwan investment from the balance of payments and employment that Systek had originally expected *with* the investment.

What Would Have Happened Without the Investment (and if the Environmental Basis on Which the Decision Was Made Had Not Changed)?

The trade flows related to this investment swamp the financial flows, so the key factor to estimate is what would have happened to Systek's U.S. market for automotive radios if the Taiwan plant had not been built. We considered three alternatives, the first two of which Systek considered and rejected in 1968:

(1) *Further automate the radio assembly process.* This was unlikely to reduce drastically the manufacturing costs. Many printed circuit boards made by Systek in the United States were already assembled automatically, and the other major manufacturing step, final assembly, had not been automated successfully.

(2) *Move the U.S. plant to a lower cost labor area in the South.* This step was taken in 1971, with a resulting saving of about 70 cents per hour in direct labor costs. However, we do not believe that this is a permanent solution, for a foreign producer located in Taiwan would have direct labor costs approximately $2.00 per hour less than in the South, as well as having lower costs of indirect labor and materials. These savings, in the case of the four products made by Systek-Taiwan, result in overall cost savings of from 5 percent to 30 percent of the factory selling price of the product, after the costs of shipping and duty are considered. Here is an example of such a cost comparison for the AM radio used in foreign automobiles:

	Costs per Unit (dollars)	
	U.S. Costs	Taiwan Costs
Direct labor	1.92	.12
Material	15.35	15.35
Labor costs and factory overhead	4.32	.67
Subtotal	21.59	16.14
Selling and administration	1.44	.88
Subtotal	23.03	17.02
Shipping and duty	0	2.22
Total cost, delivered to U.S.	23.03	19.24

However, the picture is not quite so unfavorable for a U.S. plant, because other factors tend to reduce the importance of the cost advantage shown for the foreign plant. An automobile manufacturer buying radios is concerned not only with price but with quality, promptness of delivery, stability of the source of supply, vendor innovations, and other intangibles. Although these have worked in favor of domestic producers in the past, their value is declining because the difference in quality and design capabilities is now very small; worries over delivery and stability of the source have been reduced by the greater experience of U.S. buyers with offshore sources and the risk-reducing possibilities of having multiple sources in different low-cost labor areas. Systek, by being an outside source of supply to an auto manufacturer, does not have the favored status that the electronics subsidiaries of auto companies enjoy. Hence, any price premium that might be obtained over a foreign competitor is likely to be small, or possibly nonexistent.

Other U.S. manufacturers of auto radios face a similar cost situation, and almost all of them have decided to set up plants in low-cost labor areas outside the United States; General Motors is the only automotive manufacturer with facilities to manufacture radios that does not have a radio manufacturing facility in such a low-cost labor area. The share of automobile radio production going to the offshore plants of U.S. firms has grown rapidly, although precise data are not available.[11]

If these U.S.-owned offshore plants had not existed, we believe that foreign-owned plants would have been producing many more radios for the U.S. market. Since there are only a few major customers for auto radios, the market is easy to identify and contact, and Systek found that the U.S. auto companies had received bids from foreign producers; U.S. firms were competing successfully only on the basis of offshore production. An analysis of data on production and trade in all radios and in television receivers lends some support to this belief.

Table 5-6 shows the deterioration in the U.S. competitive position in radios. Imports, since first reaching the level of one million units annually in 1956, have climbed steadily, reaching a higher percentage of U.S. consumption each successive year (column 6 of Table 5-6). By 1966 the figure was 57 percent and by 1970, 75 percent. Over 90 percent of these imports came from the Far East, with Japan being the main supplier in 1960, but beginning to share this role with other Far Eastern countries by 1970 (Table 5-7). Import data are not available on the different categories of radios: table, clock, portable, and automotive. But discussions with managers in the electronics industries indicate that in some product lines imports are much higher than 75 percent. When imports begin to take

---

[11] This is the view of a Systek International executive.

TABLE 5-6

SELECTED DATA FOR U.S. RADIO MARKET, 1925–1970

(millions of units, except columns 1 and 6)

Year	U.S. pro-duction	Imports sold with a U.S. manufactur-er's label	Imports sold with a foreign firm's label	Apparent consumption ignoring exports	Imports as a share of apparent consumption (percent)
(1)	(2)	(3)	(4)	(5)	(6)
1925	2	—	—	2	—
1930	4	—	—	4	—
1935	6	—	—	6	—
1940	12	—	—	12	—
1946	16	—	—	16	—
1948	17	—	—	17	—
1950	13	—	—	13	—
1952	10	—	—	10	—
1954	10	—	—	10	—
1956	14	—	1	15	7
1958	12	—	3	15	25

1960	17	—	8	25	32
1962	19	—	13	32	41
1964	18	1	13	32	44
1966	19	5	20	44	57
1968	17	6	24	47	64
1970	11	5	28	44	75

— = Believed to be negligible.

NOTES:

Column 2: Total radio production. SOURCE: Electronic Industries Association, *Electronic Market Data Book 1971* (Washington, D.C., 1971) and Electronic Industries Association, *Electronic Market Data Book 1969* (Washington, D.C., 1969), p. 14, minus domestic label imports (see below). Figures include auto radios.

Column 3: Includes units made in both U.S.-owned factories and non-U.S.-owned factories. Electronic Industries Association, *Electronic Market Data Book 1971* p. 18. No data available for auto radios.

Column 4: Made in non-U.S.-owned factories. Electronic Industries Association, *Electronic Market Data Book 1971*, p. 18. No data available before 1950, but presumably small. Includes auto radios.

Column 5: Total of columns (2), (3), and (4); that is, U.S. production plus U.S. imports; this assumes exports were negligible; this seems to be a reasonable assumption, for the U.S. Bureau of Commerce, *Foreign Trade Report 410*, reveals no exports in excess of 5 percent of U.S. production.

Column 6: Columns (3) plus (4) as a percentage of column (5).

TABLE 5-7
U.S. IMPORTS OF RADIOS FROM SELECTED COUNTRIES,
1960 AND 1970
(percentage of units)

Country or Area	1960 [a]	1970 [b]
Canada	—	3
Western Europe	4	1
Latin America	—	—
Japan	95	46
Other Far East	1	51
Other	—	—
Total	100	100 [c]

[a] Includes import categories 7100110, 7100130, 7100150 and 7100230.

[b] Includes import categories 7242020, 7242040, 7242050, 7242060 and 7242065.

[c] Column does not total due to rounding.

SOURCE: U.S. Bureau of the Census, *U.S. Imports of Merchandise for Consumption, Commodity by Country of Origin, Report FT 110* (Washington, D.C., Superintendent of Documents, 1960), and U.S. Bureau of the Census, *U.S. imports—General and Consumption, Schedule A Commodity and Country, Report FT 135* (Washington, D.C.: Superintendent of Documents, Dec. 1970).

over a market, they do it quickly; and imports of automotive radios have become important.

Table 5-8 gives a different view of the U.S. weakness in the world radio arena. The U.S. share of world production dropped from 51 percent in 1953 to 29 percent in 1963 and 22 percent in 1968. This fall is parallel with the rise in production in the Far East.

The television industry presents another picture of growing U.S. weakness in consumer electronics. Imports of monochrome (black-and-white) television receivers, which are somewhat similar in technology to radios, began in the early 1960s and reached 52 percent by 1970, taking only six years to go from 8 percent of the U.S. market to over 50 percent (Table 5-9). This compares with a ten-year

TABLE 5-8

PRODUCTION OF RADIOS IN SELECTED COUNTRIES,

1953, 1963, and 1968

(percentage of units)

Country or Area	1953	1963	1968
United States	50.9	29.1	21.6
European Economic Community countries	18.7 [a]	15.0	12.7
United Kingdom	4.5	4.5	1.9
Japan	5.4	28.9	37.4
Taiwan	—	—	4.4
South Korea	—	.3	1.3
India	.2	.7	1.5
World total	100.0	100.0	100.0

[a] Estimated on the assumption that Belgium had the same share of production of EEC countries in 1953 as in 1963.

SOURCE: U.N. Department of Economic and Social Affairs, *Statistical Yearbook, 1970* (New York: United Nations, 1971), p. 317.

period for radios, starting in the mid-1950s.[12] Again, as with radios, the Far East is the main supplier of imported television receivers, though Latin America, principally Mexico, has begun to cut out a niche in the market (Table 5-10). Also, as with radios, the U.S. share of world production has declined steadily (Table 5-11). These last two tables include color television, since data for black-and-white sets only are not available.

Another important trend emerges from Tables 5-6 and 5-9. Imports by U.S. manufacturers lagged considerably behind those of foreign manufacturers in radios but a little less so in monochrome television receivers. Thus it appears that competitive imports manufactured by foreign

[12] This is similar in concept to the finding that with every advancing decade the production imitation lag among countries in the world petrochemical industry drops by 40 percent; see Robert B. Stobaugh, "The Product Life Cycle and International Trade and Investment," unpublished D.B.A. thesis, Harvard University Graduate School of Business Administration, 1968, Chapter 4.

TABLE 5-9

SELECTED DATA FOR THE U.S. TELEVISION RECEIVER MARKET (MONOCHROME), 1948–1970

(millions of units, except columns 1 and 6)

Year	U.S. produc- tion	Imports sold with a U.S. manufacturer's label	Imports sold with a foreign firm's label	Apparent consumption, ignoring exports	Imports as a share of apparent consumption (percent)
(1)	(2)	(3)	(4)	(5)	(6)
1948	1.0	—	—	1.0	—
1950	7.4	—	—	7.4	—
1952	6.2	—	—	6.2	—
1954	7.4	—	—	7.4	—
1956	7.4	—	—	7.4	—
1958	5.1	—	—	5.1	—
1960	5.7	—	—	5.7	—
1962	6.5	—	.1	6.6	2

1964	7.6	.4	.3	8.3	8
1966	6.3	1.0	.5	7.8	19
1968	5.0	.8	1.2	7.0	29
1970	3.3	1.4	2.2	6.9	52

— = Believed to be negligible.

NOTES:

Column 2. Factory Production of Television Receivers, Domestic Label. SOURCE: Electronic Industries Association, *Electronic Market Data Book 1971* (Washington, D.C., 1971), p. 5, minus Domestic Label Imports (see below).

Column 3. Total Imports of Television Receivers. SOURCE: U.S. Bureau of the Census, *U.S. Imports—General and Consumption, Schedule A Commodity and Country, Report FT135* (Washington, D.C.: Superintendent of Documents, various years), minus Foreign Label Imports (see below); numbers in column 3 include units made in both U.S.-owned factories and non-U.S.-owned factories.

Column 4. SOURCE: Electronic Industries Association, *Electronic Market Data Book 1971*, p. 6; numbers in column 4 represent units made in non-U.S.-owned factories.

Column 5. Total of columns (2), (3) and (4); that is, U.S. production plus U.S. imports. Because data for exports are available only for monochrome and color combined, they were ignored, but they were so small that including them would not have affected the conclusions.

Column 6. Columns (3) plus (4) as a percentage of column (5).

TABLE 5-10

U.S. IMPORTS OF TELEVISION RECEIVERS FROM
SELECTED COUNTRIES, 1965 AND 1970

(percentage of units)

Country or Area	1965[a]	1970[a]
Canada	—	1
Western Europe	—	—
Latin America	—	6
Japan	99+	73
Other Far East	—	20
Other	—	—
Total	100[b]	100

— = Believed to be negligible.

[a] Based on import class 7241000.

[b] Column does not total due to rounding.

SOURCE: U.S. Bureau of the Census, *U.S. Imports of Merchandise for Consumption, Report FT125* (Washington, D.C.: Superintendent of Documents, December 1965), p. 158, and U.S. Bureau of the Census, *U.S. Imports—General and Consumption, Schedule A, Commodity and Country* (Washington, D.C.: Superintendent of Documents, December 1970), pp. 2–180.

rivals forced U.S. radio and television manufacturers to begin importing; however, U.S. manufacturers are becoming more willing to move quickly abroad in an attempt to retain a greater share of the U.S. market. The move abroad in automotive radios occurred about the time that foreign manufacturers began to make competitive bids, but before they had captured any important share of the U.S. market; this also is consistent with the view that the U.S. manufacturers are advancing along the "learning curve" in terms of knowing when to go overseas to fight foreign competition. And in the electronics industry, the foreign companies are large enough to effectively challenge the U.S. companies. Only four U.S. companies are in the top ten electronics companies as measured by worldwide

TABLE 5-11

PRODUCTION OF TELEVISION RECEIVERS IN SELECTED COUNTRIES,
1953, 1963, AND 1968

(percentage of units)

Country or Area	1953	1963	1968
United States	76.3	30.4	26.3
European Economic			
Community countries	1.7 [a]	17.3	15.1
United Kingdom	12.9	6.5	5.0
Japan	.2	19.4	22.9
Taiwan	—	—	1.6
South Korea	—	—	.1
India	N.A.	N.A.	N.A.
World total	100.0	100.0	100.0

— = Believed to be neglible.

[a] Estimated on the assumption that production in France and West Germany were the same percentage of total production of all EEC countries in 1953 as in 1963.

SOURCE: U.N. Department of Economic and Social Affairs, *Statistical Yearbook, 1970* (New York: United Nations, 1971), p. 318.

sales,[13] and two of these U.S. companies—IBM and Western Electric—do not compete in the consumer electronics market.

This analysis of the maufacture of radios and television receivers indicates that U.S. factories on the average managed to hold on to some parts of the U.S. market for many years after imports became important. But Systek's position is not average. Its U.S. facilities would have less of a grip on the market than the U.S. radio manufacturing subsidiaries of the auto manufacturers, which most likely would continue to operate for a long period of time despite import competition. There is no scientific method by which we can estimate accurately how long it would take

---

[13] *Fortune* 500 and 300, May 1972 and August 1972.

for foreign competitors to squeeze Systek out of the U.S. automotive radio market unless the firm resorts to foreign supply. Five years seems likely, but we make no strong defense of that time period.

Whatever the time, eventually the foreign investment's effects become positive. The general conclusions remain: the investment initially has negative effects, which become positive after several years; and the trade effects far outweigh the financial flows.

Balance of Payments

The flows that Systek planned when it decided to build the Taiwan plant show a negative effect on the U.S. balance of payments in all years, rising to $20.6 million by 1974. Table 5-12 shows the overwhelming importance of imports of components and products, which total over $90 million compared, for example, with the original capital outflow of $5.9 million. These estimates were derived primarily from Systek's records, including the planned split of production between the United States and Taiwan whereby the U.S. plant continues to manufacture sizable quantities of products as the Taiwan production builds up gradually (Table 5-13). The estimates in Table 5-13 were made on the basis of incomplete company data; we assumed that Systek's total sales of automotive radios will stay constant in units, but that there will be a gradual shift from AM radios to AM/FM radios.

But if Systek had not invested in Taiwan, the estimated results are even worse for the United States. By 1974 the deficit reaches $41.3 million (Table 5-14). In this case, U.S. imports are the only item; for we estimated that foreign manufacturers gradually take over Systek's U.S. business and export complete radios to the United States

TABLE 5-12
ITEMS ESTIMATED TO BE RECORDED ON U.S. BALANCE OF PAYMENTS
AS A RESULT OF SYSTEK'S 1969 INVESTMENT IN TAIWAN,
BASED ON PROJECT PLANS, 1969–1974
(millions of dollars)

Item	1969	1970	1971	1972	1973	1974
Merchandise Exports:						
Components	.5	1.6	1.3	.8	.9	1.0
Equipment	1.1	0	0	0	0	0
Merchandise Imports:						
Components and radios	−2.6	−12.8	−15.7	−18.2	−20.1	−22.1
Service Exports:						
Dividends and interest	0	.2	.2	.2	.2	.3
Royalties	a	.2	.2	.2	.2	.2
Other services	0.1	.1	a	a	a	a
Direct Investment:						
Capital outflow	−5.9	0	0	0	0	0
Loan repayment	1.4	.9	1.0	.7	0	0
Total	−5.4	−9.8	−13.0	−16.3	−18.8	−20.6

a Less than .05.

NOTES:

Merchandise Exports: Components. Systek planned that 25 percent of the value of components would be obtained from the United States in 1969, 15 percent in 1970, 10 percent in 1971, and 5 percent thereafter.

Merchandise Exports: Equipment. Systek planned to obtain all machinery and equipment from the U.S. We assume that all other fixed assets were purchased in Taiwan, although a small amount probably came from the U.S.

Merchandise Imports: Components and radios. These consist of the total production of radios and printed circuit boards of the Taiwan plant. U.S. duty is excluded.

Service Exports: Dividends and interest. Based on Systek's plan.

Service Exports: Royalties. Based on the agreement that Systek reached with the Taiwan government and the U.S. Internal Revenue Service.

Service Exports: Other services. We calculated these from the pro-forma schedule of general and administrative expenses of the Taiwan plant. We assumed that all expenses for temporary personnel, plus one-half of the travel and communication expenses, were to be paid to the United States. We assumed that shipping costs would not be paid to the United States.

Direct Investment. Company estimates.

TABLE 5-13
ESTIMATED PRODUCTION OF SYSTEK'S U.S. AND TAIWAN PLANTS
AS ORIGINALLY PLANNED, 1969–1974
(thousands of units)

Item	1969 (4 mos)	1970	1971	1972	1973	1974
U.S. Production:						
AM printed circuit boards	290	660	530	400	270	140
AM/FM printed circuit boards	50	140	140	140	160	180
AM radios	445	1,120	1,000	900	800	700
AM/FM radios	70	230	260	290	320	350
Taiwan Production:						
AM printed circuit boards	200	800	900	1,000	1,100	1,200
AM/FM printed circuit boards	20	90	120	150	160	170
AM radios	55	340	430	500	570	640

SOURCE: Estimated by Harvard casewriter on the assumption that total sales of automotive radios will stay constant, but that there will be a gradual shift from AM to AM/FM.

rather than some radios plus PCBs for use in U.S. assembly operations.

Table 5-15 presents an estimate of the net effect of the planned results of the Taiwan investment, obtained by subtracting Table 5-14 from Table 5-12. As shown earlier in Figure 5-1, the net annual effects become positive during the third full year of plant operation (1972) and the recoupment period is four years. Except for the first year, the trade flows are so large that all other flows are trivial by comparison.

Number of U.S. Jobs

We estimated that if events had occurred as projected in Systek's 1969 plans, then the number of jobs in Systek's

TABLE 5-14
ITEMS ESTIMATED TO BE RECORDED ON U.S. BALANCE OF PAYMENTS
IF SYSTEK HAD *NOT* MADE ITS 1969 INVESTMENT
IN TAIWAN, 1969–1974
(if the environmental conditions on which Systek's decision
was made did not change)
(millions of dollars)

Item	1969	1970	1971	1972	1973	1974
Imports of radios	0	−5.1	−12.1	−20.7	−30.3	−41.3

NOTES:

We estimated that imports gradually replace U.S. production over a five-year period for the quantity and type of products made in the U.S. plant in 1969. For the U.S. production, we assumed that all components would be brought in the United States. For the imports, we estimated that:

(1) No capital outflow, dividends, royalties, or other financial flows occur, since no U.S. firm has ownership of the producing plant.
(2) Exports from the U.S. of components and equipment are negligible, because foreign electronics firms do not rely on U.S. suppliers for these goods, especially for technologically standardized products such as auto radios.
(3) Imports to the U.S. are considerably higher in value than if Systek had made the investment. Whereas Systek sent printed circuit boards from Taiwan to be finished in the United States, a foreign producer would probably send a completed radio. This raises the value of imports by approximately 100 percent for the same quantity of units. We assumed that the radios delivered in the United States have a value equal to the radios made from Systek-Taiwan components (determined from the average ratio of the value of the printed circuit boards to the value of the finished radios for the radios made in Taiwan by Systek).

automotive radio operations in the United States would have declined gradually, for a total loss of 1,163 person-years of employment in 1974, as shown in Table 5-16. This decline in U.S. jobs occurs, of course, as the production of Systek's circuit boards and radios is transferred to Taiwan, as shown in Table 5-13. All of the lost employment is in the manufacture of the radios and components, and most of these are production jobs; a relatively few

TABLE 5-15

ESTIMATED *NET* CONTRIBUTION OF SYSTEK'S 1969 INVESTMENT IN
TAIWAN TO U.S. BALANCE OF PAYMENTS, 1969–1974[a]
(if the environmental conditions on which Systek's decision
was made did not change)

(millions of dollars)

Item	1969	1970	1971	1972	1973[a]	1974
Merchandise Exports:						
Components	.5	1.6	1.3	.8	.9	1.0
Equipment	1.1	0	0	0	0	0
Merchandise Imports:						
Components and radios	−2.6	−7.7	−3.6	2.5	10.2	19.2
Service Exports:						
Dividends and interest	0	.2	.2	.2	.2	.3
Royalties	b	.2	.2	.2	.2	.2
Other services	.1	.1	b	b	b	b
Direct Investment:						
Capital outflow	−5.9	0	0	0	0	0
Loan repayment	1.4	.9	1.0	.7	0	0
Annual total	−5.4	−4.7	−.9	4.4	11.5	20.7
Cumulative	−5.4	−10.0	−11.0	−6.6	4.9	25.6

[a] Balance of payments outflow is recovered in 1973; recoupment period is
four years.
[b] Less than .05.
SOURCE: Table 5-14 subtracted from Table 5-12.

person-years of employment are gained because of the
exports of equipment.

In contrast, we estimated that if Systek had not made the
investment in Taiwan, then the number of automotive
radio jobs in the United States would have been substantially higher during the early years of the project—only 296

TABLE 5-16

U.S. EMPLOYMENT ESTIMATED TO EXIST IN SYSTEK'S AUTO RADIO
OPERATIONS WITH SYSTEK'S 1969 INVESTMENT IN TAIWAN,
BASED ON PROJECT PLANS, 1969–1974

(person-years)

Item	1969	1970	1971	1972	1973	1974
Auto Radios and Components:						
Production workers	−180[a]	−705	−784	−864	−868	−873
Other	− 63[a]	−236	−261	−288	−288	−290
Equipment:						
Production workers	33	0	0	0	0	0
Other	12	0	0	0	0	0
Totals by type of worker:						
Production workers	−147	−705	−784	−864	−868	−873
Other	− 51	−236	−261	−288	−288	−290
Grand total	−198	−941	−1,045	−1,152	−1,156	−1,163

NOTES:

All numbers are based on the changes in employment from the average levels
existing during the first eight months of 1969, when an equivalent of 2,617 jobs
existed.

Auto Radios and Components: Production workers. For auto radios, we used
Systek data for the standard direct labor hours per unit of production and the mix of
products to be made by the U.S. plant. For components, we based our projections
on the estimated U.S. exports of components plus the ratio of shipments to
production workers in electronics components. For example, for 1970 the projected level of exports of components was $1.580 million (Table 5-12). Shipments
per production worker for electronic components were approximately $23,000.[b]
The estimated number of production workers was therefore $1,580,000/$23,000 =
69.

Auto Radios and Components: Other. We estimated these from the ratio of
production workers to other employees for the relevant SIC category (e.g., for auto
radios, we used SIC 36511—household and auto radios[c]—and our results checked
closely with Systek manning tables).

We based our estimates for equipment on similar data, using the averages for SIC
categories 35, 36, and 38 (electrical and nonelectrical machinery, instruments, and
related products).

[a] Last four months of 1969.

(Continued on next page.)

person-years of employment would have been lost in 1970, for example, compared with 941 person-years estimated for the case in which Systek invested. The difference, of course, is that no production would have been transferred out of the United States. However, we estimated that under the "no investment" case the number of jobs would begin to fall in 1970 as foreign competitors began to capture the U.S. market, completely eliminating U.S. jobs by 1974. Table 5-17 shows these projections.

Thus, the estimated net effect of the Taiwan investment is to reduce the number of U.S. jobs in the early years of the project but increase them in the later years. As shown in Table 5-18, we estimate that an annual deficit of 645 person-years of employment in 1970 becomes positive in 1972 and reaches an annual level of 1,454 in 1974. It must be remembered though, that these results are based on a comparison of two hypothetical situations: the operations of the investment as planned compared with no investment at all.

The net cumulative amount of U.S. employment after five years resulting from the investment is 1,110 person-years, most of which are in the manufacture of components and the assembly, testing, and packaging of the final product.

Skill Level of U.S. Jobs

The 1,110 person-years of employment that we estimated would be created from 1969 through 1974 as a net result of

---

[b] An average figure for components not elsewhere classified (resistors, capacitors, etc.), U.S. Bureau of the Census, *Census of Manufactures, 1967* (Washington, D.C.: Superintendent of Documents, 1971), Vol. 11, Industry Statistics, Part 3, p. 36 D-51.

[c] U.S. Bureau of the Census, *Census of Manufactures, 1967* (Washington, D.C.: Superintendent of Documents, 1971), Vol. 11, Industry Statistics, Part 3, p. 36 D-50, SIC 36511, and other relevant pages.

TABLE 5-17

U.S. EMPLOYMENT ESTIMATED TO EXIST IN SYSTEK'S AUTO RADIO
OPERATIONS IF SYSTEK HAD *NOT* MADE ITS 1969 INVESTMENT
IN TAIWAN, 1969–1974
(if the environmental conditions on which Systek's decision
was made did not change)
(person-years)

Item	1969	1970	1971	1972	1973	1974
Auto Radios and Components:						
Production workers	0	−221	−549	−963	−1,446	−1,988
Other	0	−75	−157	−289	−448	−629
Total	0	−296	−706	−1,252	−1,894	−2,617

NOTES:
All numbers are based on the estimated changes in employment from the average levels existing during the first eight months of 1969, when an equivalent of
2,617 jobs existed.
We estimated that imports would gradually replace U.S. production over a
five-year period for the quantity and type of products made in the U.S. plant in
1969. For the U.S production, we assumed that:
  (1) All components would be bought in the United States.
  (2) The same number of workers would be used to produce an equivalent
      quantity of components and radios in the United States as was
      planned by Systek for Taiwan.
  (3) The same amount of equipment used by Systek in Taiwan would be
      used in the United States for the same quantity of production.
For the imports we estimated that exports of components and equipment from
the U.S. are negligible, because foreign electronics firms do not rely on U.S.
suppliers for technologically standardized products such as auto radios.

the Taiwan investment contain a substantially greater share
of professional jobs than exist on the average for all U. S.
manufacturing—40 percent versus 15 percent (Table 5-19).
However, this figure of 40 percent was obtained by using an
average skill mix for the U.S. electronics industry, whereas
the manufacture of components and the assembly, testing,
and packaging operations—that is, the jobs estimated to be
created in the United States by the Systek investment—
probably contain a lower proportion of professional jobs.

TABLE 5-18

ESTIMATED *NET* CONTRIBUTION OF SYSTEK'S 1969 EXPANSION IN
TAIWAN TO U.S. EMPLOYMENT, 1969–1974
(if the environmental conditions on which Systek's decision
was made had not changed)
(person-years)

Item	1969	1970	1971	1972	1973	1974[a]
Auto Radios and Components:						
Production workers	−180	−484	−235	99	578	1,115
Other	− 63	−161	−104	1	160	339
Equipment:						
Production workers	33	0	0	0	0	0
Other	12	0	0	0	0	0
Totals:						
Production workers	−147	−484	−235	99	578	1,115
Other	− 51	−161	−104	1	160	339
Annual total	−198	−645	−339	100	738	1,454
Cumulative	−198	−843	−1,182	−1,082	−344	1,110

[a] Employment loss is recovered in 1974; recoupment period is five years.
SOURCE: Table 5-17 subtracted from Table 5-16.

However, for lack of better data we used the industry average; and if these estimates are correct, then the total of the two highest skilled categories—professionals and skilled—in the created jobs is 55 percent compared with only 34 percent in the average for all U.S. manufacturing. Even if our estimate of the proportion of professionals were too high by 100 percent, the two highest skill levels still would constitute a higher proportion of the created jobs than the average for all U.S. manufacturing.

* * * * *

This case, too, is consistent with the Hufbauer-Adler model in that flows connected with trade have a more

TABLE 5-19
NET EFFECT OF SYSTEK'S 1969 INVESTMENT IN TAIWAN ON U.S.
SKILL LEVELS FOR FIRST SIX MONTHS OF PROJECT COMPARED
WITH AVERAGE OF ALL U.S. MANUFACTURING [a]

	Mix of job skills (percent)	
	Created because of investment in Taiwan[b]	Average for U.S. manufacturing[c]
Professionals	40	15
Skilled	15	19
Clerical and sales	4	16
Semi and unskilled	41	50
Total	100	100
Two highest skill levels[d]	55	34
Two lowest skill levels	45	66

[a] On the assumption that the Taiwan plant operated as originally planned by Systek and that environmental conditions were as judged by Systek at the time of their investment decision.

[b] Estimated as average for SIC 363, 3641-2, and 365 for the radios and components and SIC 35, 36, and 38 for equipment. SOURCE: U.S. Bureau of the Census, *Census of Manufactures, 1967* (Washington, D.C.: Superintendent of Documents, 1971), Vol. 11, Industry Statistics, Part 3, p. 36-6, SIC 363; p. 36-7, SIC 365; p. 36C-10, SIC 3641-2; p. 35-5, SIC 35; p. 36-3, SIC 36; p. 38-2, SIC 38.

[c] Bureau of Labor Statistics, U.S. Department of Labor, *Tomorrow's Manpower Needs,* Vol. VI, revised 1971, Bulletin 1737 (Washngton, D.C.: U.S. Government Printing Office, 1972), pp. 33–35.

[d] Defined as "professionals and skilled."

important effect on the U.S. balance of payments than do other fund flows.[14] And, not unexpectedly, we estimate that trade flows are the source of most employment.

However, this case deviates from the Hufbauer-Adler model in that we estimate that U.S. imports from the U.S.

[14] G. C. Hufbauer and F. M. Adler, *Overseas Manufacturing Investments and the Balance of Payments* (Washington, D.C.: U.S. Treasury Department, 1968), Chapter 5.

subsidiary in Taiwan are less than the U.S. imports would be from competing foreign producers.[15] Also, the case illustrates a theme that runs through our other cases and that parts company with the Hufbauer-Adler assumptions: Firms competing against the output of plants owned by U.S. multinational enterprises in less-developed countries are primarily foreign firms headquartered in Japan or Europe rather than local firms headquartered in less-developed countries.

The case is useful in depicting some of the richness that exists in the real world:

(1)   Multinational enterprises, even those experienced in international business, are not run as one "economic person," but rather as a collection of organizations among which there is considerable negotiation about such matters as investment decisions.

(2)   Pressure is needed on some decision makers before they will decide to invest abroad. In this case the management of Systek's Consumer Electronics Division agreed to the building of the Taiwan plant only when forced to do so by the increasing foreign competition.

(3)   Events sometimes do not occur as predicted, and, in fact, the results of a foreign direct investment can differ very substantially from those planned.

A POSTSCRIPT SHOWING THE ACTUAL RESULTS FOR
THE FIRST YEAR AND A HALF OF
OPERATIONS OF THE PLANT

Table 5-20 shows the items actually recorded on the U.S. balance of payments as a result of Systek's Taiwan investment; 1970 is the last complete year for which we have information. The main difference between these re-

---

[15] Ibid., p. 32.

TABLE 5-20

ITEMS RECORDED ON U.S. BALANCE OF PAYMENTS AS A RESULT OF
SYSTEK'S 1969 INVESTMENT IN TAIWAN,
ACTUAL RESULTS, 1969–1970

(millions of dollars)

Item	1969	1970
Merchandise Exports:		
Components	0	1.23
Equipment	1.14	0
Merchandise Imports:		
Components and radios	0	−8.38
Service Exports:		
Dividends and interest	0	.11
Royalties	0	.11
Other services	.07	.67
Direct Investment:		
Capital outflow	−5.90	0
Loan repayment	1.44	.85
Total	−3.25	−5.42

NOTES:
Explanations are as given for Table 5-12; except since plant operations did not begin until 1970, merchandise exports and imports (other than equipment) were zero in 1969.

sults and those shown in Table 5-12 for the planned case is that the plant actually began operation in 1970 rather than in 1969 as anticipated.

On the other hand, we estimate that if Systek had *not* made the Taiwan investment, then there would *not* have been any balance-of-payments flows, for with the downturn in the U.S. economy, Systek (or other U.S. producers) would have been more likely than foreigners to supply the U.S. demand. Because U.S. companies had excess capacity, thereby making marginal costs low, it was difficult for foreign plants to capture sales. Foreign plants can more easily increase their market shares in the United States in a period of market growth than in a time of retrenchment; this was true, for example, in imports of black-and-white television receivers.[16] Foreign penetration of the U.S. auto radio market was probably slowed during the recession period. The experience of Systek adds weight to this argument. As Systek's sales dropped off because of the U.S. economic downturn, production was transferred from the Taiwan plant back to the United States, thus tending to stabilize U.S. production at the expense of that in Taiwan.

Therefore, the flows shown in Table 5-20 represent the actual *net* effects of the Taiwan investment as well as the recorded flows. The flows are negative in each year, $3.25 million in 1969 and $5.42 million in 1970.

Table 5-21 shows a comparison of these actual net effects with those net effects that we estimated earlier in this chapter if the planned results had occurred. The actual results were $2.11 million more positive during the first year than planned and $.76 million less positive during the second year. We have no results for the subsequent years. Without knowledge of the output of Systek's new plant in the southern part of the United States, it is difficult to make even a good guess. However, if Systek is able to retain its share of the U.S. market with its southern plant, then the balance-of-payments effects of the Taiwan investment depend primarily on receipts of dividends and interests, royalties, payments for other services, and repayment of the loan as shown in Table 5-12. A scanning of

---

[16] Robert B. Stobaugh, "A Study of Economic Conditions in the United States Television Receiver Industry for United States Tariff Commission Investigation, No. TEA-I-21," October 1971, pp. 7, 19.

TABLE 5-21
ESTIMATED *NET* EFFECTS OF SYSTEK'S 1969 TAIWAN INVESTMENT
ON U.S. BALANCE OF PAYMENTS, ACTUAL RESULTS VERSUS
PLANNED RESULTS, 1969–1970
(millions of dollars)

	1969	1970
Actual results	−3.25	−5.42
Planned results	−5.36	−4.66
Difference	2.11	−.76

SOURCE: Tables 5-15 and 5-20.

Tables 5-12 and 5-20 suggests that these flows would offset the total outflows of $8.67 million ($3.25 plus $5.42) recorded in 1969–1970 by perhaps 1977 or so, resulting in a recoupment period of some eight years, instead of the four years estimated according to Systek's plans.

Thus we conclude that the 1970 recession probably delayed the recoupment period for the balance of payments up to perhaps eight years; but this latter estimate contains a high degree of uncertainty.

Our estimates of the actual effects of the Taiwan investment on U.S. employment are somewhat consistent with the balance-of-payments effects. During 1969 and 1970 the estimated net effects of the investment were somewhat more positive than under the planned conditions (Tables 5-22 through 5-25).

Table 5-22 shows the U.S. employment that actually existed during 1969 and 1970 with the Taiwan plant investment. These figures are lower than the planned results in Table 5-16 because of the drop in U.S. busine ss.

Table 5-23 shows the U.S. employment that would have existed without the Systek plant but with the recession that took place in the United States. In this case the

TABLE 5-22

U.S. EMPLOYMENT IN SYSTEK'S AUTO RADIO OPERATIONS WITH
SYSTEK'S 1969 INVESTMENT IN TAIWAN,
ACTUAL RESULTS, 1969–1970
(person-years)

Item	1969	1970
Auto Radios and Components:		
Production workers	−203	−734
Other	− 72	−249
Equipment:		
Production workers	33	0
Other	12	0
Totals:		
Production workers	−170	−734
Other	− 60	−249
Grand total	−230	−983

NOTE:
Explanations are as given for Table 5-16.

employment level for 1969 was the same as the actual
case, for the plant did not start operations until 1970.
However, in 1970, U.S. employment without the Taiwan
plant would have been higher than the actual case.

Table 5-24 shows the net effect of the Taiwan investment, which was obtained by subtracting the estimated
results without the investment (Table 5-23) from the actual
results with the investment (Table 5-22). Even though the
existence of the plant caused a loss of 643 person-years of
employment that would otherwise have existed, the delay
in starting up the plant caused the combined results for the
two years to be more favorable under the actual case than
under the planned case, as shown in Table 5-25. But

TABLE 5-23

U.S. EMPLOYMENT IN SYSTEK'S AUTO RADIO OPERATIONS
ESTIMATED TO EXIST IF TAIWAN HAD *NOT* MADE
ITS 1969 INVESTMENT IN TAIWAN, 1969–1970
(with actual environmental conditions)

(person-years)

Item	1969	1970
Auto Radios and Components:		
Production workers	−203	−252
Other	− 72	− 88
Equipment:		
Production workers	33	0
Other	12	0
Totals:		
Production workers	−170	−252
Other	− 60	− 88
Grand total	−230	−340

NOTE:
All numbers are based on the changes in employment from the average levels existing during the first eight months of 1969. Explanations are as given for Table 5-17; except employment in 1969 was the same as with the investment (Table 5-22) because the plant did not begin operation until 1970. For 1970, we estimated that Systek would have lowered prices sufficiently to keep U.S. business, and thus imports were zero.

whether the plant actually makes a positive contribution to U.S. employment depends on its role in helping to combat foreign competition that might have developed after the 1970 recession. Thus, our conclusions about the actual effect of the Taiwan plant on U.S. employment are even less certain than our conclusions on the balance of payments.

TABLE 5-24

ESTIMATED *NET* CONTRIBUTION OF SYSTEK'S 1969 INVESTMENT
IN TAIWAN TO U.S. EMPLOYMENT, 1969–1970
(with actual environmental conditions)
(person-years)

Item	1969	1970
Auto Radios and Components:		
Production workers	0	−482
Other	0	−161
Equipment:		
Production workers	0	0
Other	0	0
Totals:		
Production workers	0	−482
Other	0	−161
Grand total	0	−643

SOURCE: Table 5-23 subtracted from Table 5-22.

TABLE 5-25

ESTIMATED *NET* EFFECTS OF SYSTEK'S TAIWAN INVESTMENT ON
ACTUAL U.S. EMPLOYMENT, ACTUAL RESULTS VERSUS
PLANNED RESULTS, 1969–1970
(person-years)

	1969	1970
Actual results	0	−643
Planned results	−198	−645
Margin of actual results over planned results	198	2

SOURCE: Tables 5-18 and 5-24.

6

The Pattern
of the Future?
Farm Machinery
Manufacture
in Europe

By the late 1960's. . . . . U.S. parents [of multinational enterprises] were better equipped than they had ever been to evaluate foreign opportunities and assess foreign threats, and to respond to these opportunities and threats by developing complex logistical networks among their affiliates.[1]

THE EUROPEAN EXPANSION IN THE MID-1960s of a U.S.-based manufacturer of farm machinery, which we call by the disguised name of the American Tractor Company, was part of the company's development of a complex logistical net-

---

[1] Raymond Vernon, *Sovereignty at Bay* (New York: Basic Books, 1971), p. 107.

work to provide tractors from several factories for many markets. This expansion was the culmination of an evolutionary process that started when American Tractor Company (ATC) began expanding abroad in the 1950s.

In 1956 ATC purchased a German company in order to secure a manufacturing and selling base which might serve the European Economic Community (EEC) market once the EEC was formed, but this did not happen. The German subsidiary continued to manufacture the same tractors it had produced before the purchase; these tractors were sold primarily in Germany. A few years later, ATC started a French subsidiary to assemble tractors for the French market.

By 1963 the ATC international manufacturing policy veered in a new direction. The firm decided that the two EEC plants would complement one another and would be operated as though they were one. They were to manufacture products for all of the EEC and also export to non-EEC markets. The plans were as follows: (1) a new line of low horsepower tractors, first introduced in the United States in 1960 and designed for worldwide markets, would be manufactured; (2) both plants would be modernized and expanded; (3) both plants would specialize in the manufacture of parts—engines and transmissions in France and castings and body components in Germany, for example; and (4) Germany would assemble tractors.

For these investments an appropriation request was approved by the board of directors. We do not have access to this request. But we do know that ATC considered a number of factors in making the decision.

First, at the same levels of production, manufacturing costs in Continental Europe and the United Kingdom for tractors of all sizes were lower than in the United States, by some 25 percent; Table 6-1 shows a comparison of U.S. and

TABLE 6-1
COMPARISON OF U.S. AND U.K. TRACTOR MANUFACTURING COSTS
AT 60,000 UNITS OF ANNUAL OUTPUT, BY SIZE OF TRACTOR, 1968
(Canadian dollars)

	Cost per tractor (at 60,000 annual output)		
	40 HP	*90 HP*	*130 HP*
U.S. cost (1968)	2,812	3,746	5,061
U.K. cost (1967–68) post-devaluation	2,092	2,805	3,806
Difference: U.K. below U.S.	720	941	1,255
U.K. as percentage of U.S.	74.4%	74.9%	75.2%

SOURCE: Royal Commission on Farm Machinery, *Special Report on Prices* (Ottawa: Queen's Printer, 1969), p. 68.

U.K. costs. In addition, the EEC had a 13.4 percent tariff on tractor imports (compared with 0.4 percent in the United States).[2] And, of course, there were transportation costs from the United States to Europe, totaling about $100 for the smaller tractors and $200 for the larger ones. Since costs in Europe were lower than in the United States and output levels were comparable, world production had gradually shifted away from the United States toward Europe (Table 6-2).

Second, ATC needed a new line of tractors to help increase its rather small market share in Europe; for ATC had only 6 percent of the West German market, 5 percent of the French market, and less than 3 percent of the Italian market, compared with the 15 percent or more enjoyed by leaders in

[2] Bela Balassa, "Tariff Protection in Industrial Countries: An Evaluation," *Journal of Political Economy* (December 1965), p. 580.

TABLE 6-2

PRODUCTION OF TRACTORS IN NON-COMMUNIST WORLD,
1937, 1951, 1960

(percentage of units)

	1937	*1951*	*1960*
United States	88	70	25
United Kingdom	6	16	26
Rest of Western Europe[a]	6	10	42
Rest of world	nil[b]	4[b]	7
Total	100	100	100

[a] Primarily West Germany, France and Italy.
[b] Data not available; these are approximations by us.

NOTE:
The figures for 1960 include agricultural and nonagricultural tractors, but this inclusion does not change the main conclusions to be drawn from the table.
SOURCE: For 1937 and 1951, Royal Commission on Farm Machinery, *Special Report on Prices* (Ottawa: Queen's Printer, 1969), p. 8. For 1960, U.N. Department of Economic and Social Affairs, *The Growth of World Industry, 1970 Edition* (New York: United Nations, 1972), Vol. 11, pp. 381–446.

the European markets and by ATC in the United States. (The leaders in Europe were Massey-Ferguson in France, Deutz and a U.S.-based firm in West Germany, and Fiat in Italy.)[3] Market share is important because of economies of scale in both distribution and production. For example, ATC data show that production costs for a 45 HP tractor are 8 percent lower at an annual output of 50,000 units than at 25,000 units. Furthermore, ATC concluded that this new

[3] *Report of the Royal Commission on Farm Machinery* (Ottawa: Information Canada, 1971), p. 132; E.P. Learned, et al., *Business Policy: Text and Cases* (Homewood, Illinois: R.D. Irwin, 1969), p. 211; and interviews with several companies.

line should be a full one to enable ATC to be completely competitive in marketing.[4]

Given the intrinsically lower European costs and the strong need of ATC for a new line of small tractors in Europe, ATC believed it made sense to build them in Europe. Furthermore, this could be done without idling any U.S. facilities, for the growth in the U.S. market was resulting in a need for even more U.S. facilities.[5]

Given these rationales for producing in Europe, it was only natural that ATC management viewed their European investments as a major step in their drive to offer a complete line of tractors worldwide. The French-German facilities were to be ATC's low-cost source of standard small HP tractors, which ATC defined as not exceeding 77 HP. Europe was to export these tractors to other countries having tariff barriers sufficiently low to allow imports. The United States, on the other hand, was to continue to be a partial supplier of certain specialized small HP tractors to markets other than Europe and the major supplier of large HP tractors to all markets.

ATC invested $54.4 million for this European expansion in the mid-1960s. Various segments of the plants were completed in 1964 and the entire program was completed by 1966.

We were not given permission to publish income statements and balance sheets of the European subsidiaries. However, we know that most of the $54.4 million was spent in 1965; for convenience, we assume in our analysis that all

---

[4] This conclusion is consistent with published data showing that manufacturers with a full line of tractors typically had much larger market shares than manufacturers with limited lines. E.P. Learned, et al., *Business Policy,* p. 216.

[5] In fact, ATC's annual reports show that it spent about $200 million for new capacity in Canada and the United States in the late 1960s.

of this expenditure was in 1965 and refer to this expansion as the "1965 expansion." Of the $54.4 million, ATC invested $21.3 million in France and $33.1 million in Germany; part of each investment was equity and part was a loan.

This case differs from the other cases in this book because our estimate of what occurred with the investment is based on actual experience rather than projected results; and, as will become evident, we imagine that the experience was substantially different from the projections.

The first few years of operations were not so bad. In 1966 and 1967 ATC engaged in a number of separate transactions, which resulted in a net outflow of $3.1 million in new funds to the French-German operation (a $25.0 million net outflow in 1966 partially offset by a $21.9 million net inflow in 1967, Table 6-3).

But the results of the operations in the period 1968 through 1970 necessitated a flood of fresh funds from the United States—a net of some $67.9 million, mostly to Germany. Altogether, through 1970 ATC had some $125 million invested in their 1965 European expansion. In 1970, the latest year for which we have data, the French operation was operating at a profit but the German operation still showed a loss.

In retrospect it is easy to see the reason for the losses. The European market for tractors grew less than ATC had anticipated. As a result, production of tractors in Europe grew only 2 percent annually from 1964 through 1969 and actually declined in West Germany from 1967 through 1969.[6] Excess capacity was widespread in Europe during the latter part of the 1960s and competition was quite severe. ATC operated its West German factory at only 72 percent of its rated capacity.

---

[6] U.N. Department of Economic and Social Affairs, *The Growth of World Industry, 1970 Edition* (New York: United Nations, 1972), Vol. 2, pp. 381, 446.

TABLE 6-3

FINANCIAL FLOWS TO AND FROM THE U.S. PARENT AS A RESULT OF
AMERICAN TRACTOR COMPANY'S 1965 EXPANSION IN
EUROPE, 1965–1970

(millions of dollars)

	1965	1966	1967	1968	1969	1970
OUTFLOWS						
Equity:						
To France	− 9.9	0	−.8	0	0	−.1
To Germany	−24.8	0	−1.6	0	0	0
Loans:						
To France	−11.4	0	0	0	−3.8	−7.4
To Germany	− 8.3	−31.1	0	−29.1	−14.9	−21.2
Total outflows	−54.4	−31.1	−2.4	−29.1	−18.7	−28.7
INFLOWS						
Repayments:						
From France	0	5.2	4.9	6.4	0	0
From Germany	0	0	18.1	0	0	0
Interest:						
From France	0	.4	.4	.2	0	.1
From Germany	0	.1	.1	.1	0	0
Royalties and Management						
Fees: From France and						
Germany	0	.4	.8	.5	.6	.7
Total inflows	0	6.1	24.3	7.2	.6	.8
NET TOTAL	−54.4	−25.0	21.9	−21.9	−18.1	−27.9

SOURCE: Company records.

Although our analysis is not designed to determine
whether the investment was satisfactory from ATC's viewpoint, this question quickly pops to the surface. If the
analysis stopped where the data do, that is, 1970, the
inclination would be to conclude that the investment in-

deed was not satisfactory. But before closing the door on that question, two other factors must be considered.

First, ATC realized some profits on its extra U.S. exports made as a result of the French-German expansion, and we don't know how much this incremental profit was. But we know that the quantity of the exports was substantial. ATC's records show that from 1965 through 1970 the company exported some $200 million worth of tractors, components, and material to France and Germany and over $100 million worth of tractors to the rest of the world (Table 6-4). Some of those were exports of large tractors and hence would have little or no competition from factories in Europe. But given the freight and duty plus differences between European and U.S. costs, the sales of small tractors almost surely represented a book loss and perhaps even an out-of-pocket loss.

Second, over the long run the European expansion might enable ATC to increase its competitiveness in Europe and worldwide and hence, in the 1970s, put the company in a better position from a profit standpoint than it would otherwise have been. Indeed, by 1971, ATC managed to increase its market share, albeit slightly, in both France and West Germany.[7]

NET EFFECTS OF THE INVESTMENT

The most striking result of our estimates showing how the 1965 French-German expansion of ATC affected the U.S. economy is that in spite of the large financial outflows experienced by ATC from 1965 through 1970, the net position of the U.S. balance of payments was positive when cumulated over these years. A positive net position was registered in four of the six years (Figure 6-1). This positive effect results from an increase in U.S. exports,

---

[7] Interviews with companies other than ATC.

TABLE 6-4

U.S. EXPORTS AND U.S. IMPORTS OF TRACTORS, MATERIAL, AND
COMPONENTS BY AMERICAN TRACTOR COMPANY, 1965–1970
(millions of dollars)

Item	1965	1966	1967	1968	1969	1970
U.S. Exports of Tractors: All sizes in anticipation of starting up new European facilities[a]	64.8	0	0	0	0	0
Others, less than 60 HP	0	7.4	12.7	13.8	17.5	20.8
Others, 60 HP or greater	0	24.3	26.7	24.0	31.7	27.3
U.S. Exports of Material and Components to:						
France	0	3.5	2.9	1.9	2.0	6.8
Germany	0	7.3	4.9	5.8	6.3	7.3
U.S. Exports of Equipment to:[b]						
France	16.0	0	0	0	0	0
Germany	3.8	0	0	0	0	0
Total U.S. Exports	84.6	42.5	47.2	45.5	57.5	62.2
Total U.S. Imports, Products from France and Germany	0	− .2	− .7	−1.1	−1.3	−2.7
Net U.S. trade balance	84.6	42.3	46.5	44.4	56.2	59.5

[a] Small and large tractors, including industrial tractors and combines, shipped in the years 1963 through 1965; for simplicity, they have been included in 1965.
[b] These occurred from 1964 through 1966, but although they were invoiced through the U.S. parent, we were unable to obtain exact timing. For simplicity, we assumed they occurred wholly in 1965.
SOURCE: Company records.

which also makes the employment impact positive in all years, especially in the first (Figure 6-2). And these additional jobs in the United States were higher in skill levels than the average for all U.S. manufacturing.

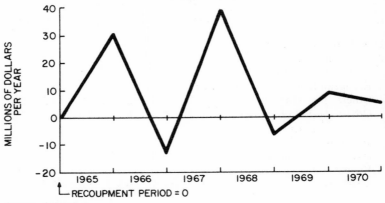

Figure 6-1

ESTIMATED NET CONTRIBUTION OF
AMERICAN TRACTOR COMPANY'S 1965 EXPANSION IN EUROPE TO
U.S. BALANCE OF PAYMENTS, 1965-1970

Source: Table 6-8

These conclusions were derived from two sets of estimates: (1) the U.S. balance of payments and employment with ATC's 1965 European expansion, and (2) the U.S. balance of payments and employment *without* the expansion, assuming that no other U.S.-owned firm could expand production outside the United States to provide tractors for the markets served by the capacity added in ATC's 1965 European expansion. The net effects of the expansion were then obtained by substracting the second estimate (the "no expansion" case) from the first estimate (the "expansion" case).

What Would Have Happened Without the Investment?

ATC's records show what happened to the U.S. balance of payments and employment *with* the expansion.

Figure 6-2

ESTIMATED NET CONTRIBUTION OF
AMERICAN TRACTOR COMPANY'S 1965 EXPANSION IN EUROPE TO
U.S. EMPLOYMENT, 1965-1970

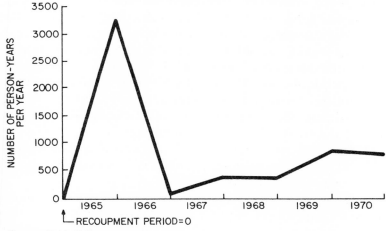

Source: Table 6-11

But to estimate what the U.S. balance of payments and employment would have been *without* the expansion necessitates a close look at ATC's European operations, competition within the European industry, and the likely effects of these factors on U.S. exports.

If ATC had *not* been allowed to expand in the EEC in the mid-1960s, then it would have had no alternative but to close its French and West German subsidiaries. Even with the expansion and introduction of a full line of new products—steps that both ATC and we believe to have improved the competitive position of their French-German operations—ATC had to put substantial funds into the operations between 1966 and 1970. Without the expansion, ATC's substantially worsened competitive position would have produced even greater losses, so even more funds would most likely have been required.

However, we assume that under the "no expansion" case ATC would not have been allowed to export these additional funds even if it had wanted to, which would have been doubtful. And it is unlikely that local sources, such as banks, would have provided the needed funds; both subsidiaries lost money in 1965 and it is doubtful that the operations would ever have been profitable again without the expansion and addition of product lines. Thus, we estimate that the French and German subsidiaries would eventually have been liquidated.

Valuing an enterprise to be liquidated is a tricky business at best, but valuing one that is losing money is an even more difficult task.

If the joint French-German enterprise were to be valued as an ongoing business, then it would be worth very little, for it did not cover its out-of-pocket costs in 1965; it almost covered out-of-pocket expenses in 1966 and 1967, but it did not do so in the years 1968 through 1970. And presumably its cash flow from 1966 onward would have been even worse without the 1965 investment.

If the joint French-German enterprise were to be valued on the basis of liquidating its assets and liabilities, several problems arise. First, how close is net book value to the market value? Fixed assets could be either undervalued or overvalued, but cut off from the know-how of the parent, a buyer might pay less than book value for the machinery; but the land, and perhaps the buildings, probably would be worth more than the book value. Inventories likely would be overvalued and even accounts receivable to some extent. Second, what year would the liquidation have taken place? In 1965, the net book value approximated a positive

$50 million. By 1970, it approximated a negative $50 million.[8]

We estimate a sales value of zero, partly because in our discussions with the management of ATC, they stated that they would have attempted to continue their French-German operations. And this continued effort would have gradually reduced the value, likely to the point that its losses would offset the worth of the land, buildings, and equipment. We recognize that others might project something more than zero, which could have a substantial impact on final estimates of the net effects of the actual investment on the U.S. balance of payments.

The question naturally arises about the ability of the non-U.S. companies to meet the needs of the markets served by the U.S.-owned factories in the EEC and United Kingdom if U.S. companies had not been allowed to expand and serve these markets. In this analysis, the EEC and U.K. factories are considered together because the output of some of these plants is rationalized, with some parts made in the EEC and others in the United Kingdom. In 1966, U.S. companies manufactured 142,300 tractors in the EEC and United Kingdom out of a total production in these two areas of 448,400. Because there were only three major U.S. tractor companies manufacturing in the EEC and United Kingdom, to state the output of the two that would continue to operate if ATC were to cease European manufacture would give away ATC's corporate identity. Thus, for analytical purposes, we assume that in 1966 ATC made 47,400 units and the other two U.S. tractor companies made 47,400 each, or 94,800 total. Therefore, the problem becomes: Could foreign tractor companies have expanded

---

[8] Company records.

to cater for the loss of ATC's output and the entire growth in
the markets served by the company's EEC and U.K. plants
if the EEC and U.K. output of the other two U.S. firms had
been held to 94,800 annually?

Table 6-5 provides the answer. The total EEC and U.K.
production rose from 448,400 units in 1966 to 548,700 in
1969, an annual increase of 7 percent; this 1969 total includes the export markets served by the EEC and U.K.
plants. With ATC's dropping out and the EEC output of
the other two U.S. firms not growing, the non-U.S. firms
would have had to increase their EEC and U.K. output
from 306,100 in 1966 to 453,900 in 1969, an annual growth
rate of 14 percent. We do not know what their actual
increase in output was from 1966 to 1969, but we judge
that they would have been capable of increasing their
production at 14 percent annually, especially since there
was some excess capacity in the EEC and U.K. Thus,
U.S. exports would not have expanded to fill any appreci-
able part of the void created by ATC's shutdown in
France and Germany and by the failure of the other U.S.
firms to expand their EEC and U.K. production. Furthermore, producers in a number of other European countries, such as Austria, Finland, Spain, and Sweden, provide competition for the EEC and U.K. factories, and
virtually none of this "other European" capacity is U.S.-
owned.

Although we do not have complete data on production
of individual firms in the rest of the world, an analysis of
available data suggests that non-U.S. firms would have
had no problem in expanding to serve the foreign markets
if U.S.-owned firms failed to do so. World production
outside the United States, EEC, and United Kingdom,
and excluding the USSR, China, and Eastern Europe, was
only about 91,000 in 1966 because many of these markets

TABLE 6-5

GROWTH IN OUTPUT REQUIRED OF NON-U.S. FIRMS IN EEC AND
U.K. TO MEET PRODUCTION REQUIREMENTS OF EEC AND U.K. IN
1969 IF AMERICAN TRACTOR COMPANY CEASED EEC PRODUCTION
AND OTHER U.S. FIRMS COULD NOT EXPAND OUTPUT IN EEC
AND U.K., 1966 TO 1969

(thousands of units)

Company	1966	1969
American Tractor Company	47.5	0
U.S.—Firm A	47.4	47.4
U.S.—Firm B	47.4	47.4
Total U.S. owned output	142.3	94.8
Massey-Ferguson[a]	111.0	
Fiat	41.5	
Renault/Porsche	19.0	
David Brown	18.5	
British Leyland	15.0	
Deutz	17.0	
Other	84.1	
Total non-U.S.-owned output	306.1	453.9
Grand total, EEC and U.K. production requirements[b]	448.4	548.7

[a] This is the European output of Massey-Ferguson. Canadian expansion is not considered because costs are similar to U.S. costs.

[b] Includes export markets served by EEC and U.K. plants.

SOURCE: All data for 1966 except the individual outputs of the U.S. firms were obtained from *Special Report on Prices of Tractors and Combines in Canada and Other Countries,* Royal Commission on Farm Machinery (Ottawa: Queen's Printer, 1969). The individual outputs of the U.S. firms in 1966 are assumed to be one-third of the total output of the U.S. firms in order to hide corporate identities. The total non-U.S.-owned output in 1969 was calculated by subtracting the total U.S.-owned output (94.8) from the Grand Total (548.7). The Grand Total in 1969 was obtained from U.N. Department of Economic and Social Affairs, *The Growth of World Industry, 1970 Edition* (New York: United Nations, 1972), Vol. 11, pp. 381, 446.

were served from EEC and U.K. plants. Since most of this 91,000 was not produced by U.S. firms, the non-U.S. firms on a worldwide basis would have had little difficulty in producing the tractors needed outside the United States in the sizes made outside the United States, that is, the smaller sized tractors.

U.S. exports of smaller tractors are not needed to serve the markets that are provided for by the European factories. But ATC exported some low-horsepower tractors, primarily to locations other than Europe, even after the start-up of the new French and German facilities. However, most of these were models not made by the ATC in the French-German facilities, which specialized in those models most popular in Europe.

ATC management assumed that if the U.S. government prevented them from expanding output or making new investments abroad, they would continue to operate the French and German facilities at their old levels of output. They assumed that they could send out loans to cover any losses. Under these conditions ATC management estimated a lower level of U.S. exports of both high- and low-horsepower tractors than in the case with the expanded French-German facilities, because ATC's worldwide distribution system would have been much weaker without the low-cost source of low-horsepower tractors in Europe. European expansion results in an increase in U.S. exports because the European-made tractors, when combined with U.S. exports, provide ATC dealers worldwide with a full line of tractors; this not only increases overall tractor sales but increases the number of ATC dealers.

Since we assume that any U.S. restrictions on foreign investment would prevent ATC from continuing to lend money to its French and German subsidiaries, which would be liquidated, we believe that ATC's worldwide distribution system, especially in Europe, would have been much weaker than under the case assumed by ATC's management. Thus, if ATC's estimates of their tractor exports are correct for their assumptions, they are too high for our assumptions. However, for lack of better estimates, we use ATC's, realizing that they might well be too high for the "no expansion" case.

Other U.S. exports would have been lost as well. European firms expanding in place of ATC would not have obtained equipment from the United States since European producers typically use European equipment; nor would they have imported components and materials from the United States as did ATC. But perhaps the most important U.S. export loss would have been the $64.8 million of products that ATC exported in 1963, 1964, and 1965 to build up its European distribution system in anticipation of starting up its new French-German facilities. There is no way of knowing with certainty that ATC would not have exported these products even without the European expansion, but there is considerable support for their statement that they would not have. Our calculations, based on confidential data from ATC's records, show that the freight, duty, and differences in manufacturing costs almost surely made these exports unprofitable on an "average cost" basis and perhaps even on a marginal cost basis; that is, unprofitable unless future profits from European operations were realized owing to the increased market penetration obtained because of these anticipatory exports. Second, ATC has not exported such a large quantity of tractors to Europe either before or since this time.

Thus, without ATC's French-German expansion, U.S. exports would have been substantially less than they actually were.

Balance of Payments

Table 6-6 shows the items recorded in U.S. balance of payments as a result of ATC's 1965 European expansion.

TABLE 6-6

ITEMS RECORDED ON U.S. BALANCE OF PAYMENTS AS A RESULT OF
AMERICAN TRACTOR COMPANY'S 1965 EXPANSION IN EUROPE,
1965–1970

(millions of dollars)

Item	1965	1966	1967	1968	1969	1970
Merchandise Exports:						
Tractors, all sizes in anticipation of European expansion[a]	64.8	0	0	0	0	0
Other tractors less than 60 HP	0	7.4	12.7	13.8	17.5	20.8
Other tractors 60 HP or greater	0	24.3	26.7	24.0	31.7	27.3
Materials and components	0	10.8	7.8	7.7	8.3	14.1
Equipment[b]	19.8	0	0	0	0	0
Merchandise Imports:						
Tractors	0	− .2	− .7	−1.1	−1.3	−2.7
Service Exports:						
Interest	0	.5	.5	.3	0	.1
Royalties and fees	0	.4	.8	.5	.6	.7
Direct Investment:						
Equity	−34.7	0	−2.4	0	0	− .1
Loans made	−19.7	−31.1	0	−29.1	−18.7	−28.6
Loans repaid	0	5.2	23.0	6.4	0	0
Total	30.2	17.3	68.4	22.5	38.1	31.6

[a] Totals for 1963–1965. We show them in 1965 for simplicity.
[b] Totals for 1964–1966, but the exact timing is not known. We show them in 1965 for simplicity.
SOURCE: Company records.

The totals are positive for all years because the large financial deficits are overcome by even larger trade flows. And within the trade flows, the U.S. exports of tractors are by far the largest group.

Table 6-7 shows the items that we estimate would have been recorded on the U.S. balance of payments if ATC had *not* expanded in Europe. Again, the totals are positive in all years, with trade flows accounting for all of the entries. And in this case, exports of tractors dominate the trade flows even more than in the actual case discussed above.

To determine the net effects of ATC's European expan-

TABLE 6-7

ITEMS ESTIMATED TO BE RECORDED ON U.S. BALANCE OF PAYMENTS IF AMERICAN TRACTOR COMPANY HAD *NOT* MADE ITS 1965 EXPANSION IN EUROPE, 1965–1970

(millions of dollars)

Item	1965	1966	1967	1968	1969	1970
Merchandise Exports:						
Tractors less than 60 HP	0	7.4	7.8	8.6	9.5	9.0
Tractors 60 HP or greater	0	23.5	22.0	21.0	20.5	20.0
Merchandise Imports:						
Tractors	0	− .2	− .7	−1.1	−1.3	−2.7
Direct Investment:						
Sale of French and German subsidiaries	0	0	0	0	0	0
Total	0	30.7	29.1	28.5	28.7	26.3

NOTES:

Merchandise Exports. Estimated by us after discussion with company and examination of certain confidential records. Rationale for each category is discussed in detail in text. These exports do not include tractors in anticipation of European expansion, which we estimated as zero.

sion, the estimated effects *without* the investment were
subtracted from the actuals *with* the investment (Table
6-8). The top row of this table shows the importance of the
so-called "anticipatory" exports, that is, the $64.8 million

TABLE 6-8

ESTIMATED *NET* EFFECTS ON U.S. BALANCE OF
PAYMENTS OF AMERICAN TRACTOR COMPANY'S 1965
EXPANSION IN EUROPE, 1965–1970

(millions of dollars)

Item	1965	1966	1967	1968	1969	1970
Merchandise Exports:						
Tractors, all sizes in anticipation of						
European expansion	64.8	0	0	0	0	0
Other tractors less than 60 HP	0	0	4.9	5.2	8.0	11.8
Other tractors 60 HP or greater	0	.8	4.7	3.0	11.2	7.3
Materials and components	0	10.8	7.8	7.7	8.3	14.1
Equipment	19.8	0	0	0	0	0
Merchandise Imports:						
Tractors	0	0	0	0	0	0
Service Exports:						
Interest	0	.5	.5	.3	0	.1
Royalties and fees	0	.4	.8	.5	.6	.7
Direct Investment:						
Equity	−34.7	0	−2.4	0	0	−0.1
Loans made	−19.7	−31.1	0	−29.1	−18.7	−28.6
Loans repaid	0	5.2	23.0	6.4	0	0
Annual totals	30.2	−13.4	39.3	−6.0	9.4	5.3
Cumulative	30.2	16.8	56.1	50.1	59.5	64.8

SOURCE: Table 6-7 subtracted from Table 6-6.

of U.S. exports of tractors in 1963, 1964, and 1965, to build up ATC's foreign distribution systems and gain market penetration prior to the start-up of the new European facilities. The next two rows show the importance of the so-called "associated" exports, that is, the incremental exports of tractors from 1966 through 1970 caused by ATC's better worldwide distribution system that resulted from their new line of low-cost, low-horsepower tractors made in their expanded European facilities. In addition, two other categories of trade were important: the export of equipment for the expansion and the export of material and components for assembly in the European plants.

Even though the direct investment flows, mostly in the form of loans to the European subsidiaries, were quite large, these outflows were offset by the even larger U.S. exports of merchandise. The net result is that we estimate the expansion had a positive effect on the U.S. balance of payments in four of the first six years, with the total positive effect over the six years being some $65 million. Of course, we do not have the records beyond 1970, and it is possible that continued financial losses by the European operations could result in large financial outflows that erode the net positive balance-of-payments effects shown in Table 6-8. But, since the net exports typically have exceeded the net financial outflows, it is likely that the net balance-of-payments effects of the investment will remain positive. If they do become negative, it will not happen for a long time.

The increased production in the United States, resulting from the European investment, boosts the efficiency of the U.S. operation because of both the increase in production experience and the static-scale economies realized through higher levels of annual production. Also, without any further expansion of U.S. output abroad, the non-U.S.

companies would expand their output even faster than they have; this expansion in turn would improve their efficiency vis-à-vis their U.S. competitors. Because of the difficulty in quantifying such effects, we ignored them in our analysis.

Number of U.S. Jobs

Because U.S. exports dominate the balance-of-payments analysis, and because of the close connection between U.S. exports and the number of U.S. jobs, it is not surprising that our employment estimates follow closely our balance-of-payments estimates. Table 6-9 shows that U.S. exports of tractors accounted for virtually all of the U.S. jobs that existed as a result of the investment. A relatively few jobs resulted from the technology and management required to service and operate the investment.

If ATC had not made the investment, then we estimate that the only U.S. jobs which would have existed are those created by trade, primarily exports (Table 6-10). As with the actual case, a few jobs would have been created to service tractors imported into the United States. The number of jobs is quite small; perhaps this is why this category of jobs is often overlooked in analyses of the effects of imports on the U.S. economy.

Table 6-11 presents our estimates of the net employment effects of the investment. A net of over 3,000 person-years of employment was created in 1963, 1964, and 1965 because of the anticipatory exports and the exports of equipment (recorded in the table under 1965). Thereafter, the employment effects continue to be positive in all years, primarily because of our estimates that the trade effects are positive in all years.

TABLE 6-9

U.S. EMPLOYMENT EXISTING AS A RESULT OF AMERICAN TRACTOR
COMPANY'S 1965 EXPANSION IN EUROPE, 1965–1970

(person-years)

Item	1965	1966	1967	1968	1969	1970
Merchandise Exports:[a]						
Tractors, all sizes in anticipation of European expansion[b]	2,467	0	0	0	0	0
Other tractors less than 60 HP	0	270	480	520	645	775
Other tractors 60 HP or greater	0	936	1,016	917	1,222	1,047
Equipment[c]	739	0	0	0	0	0
Merchandise Imports:						
Service	0	1	3	4	4	10
Service Exports:						
Technology and management	40	40	40	40	40	40
Expatriates	22	22	22	22	22	22
Total	3,268	1,269	1,561	1,503	1,933	1,894

[a] Includes materials and components as well as finished products.

[b] See note (a), Table 6-6.

[c] See note (b), Table 6-6. Number of person-years per dollar of equipment assumed to be the same as for dollar of tractor exports.

SOURCE: Company records.

Of course, as with all analyses in this book, the employment effects of the outflows of financial funds are not considered. First, we are unable to estimate how ATC would have used these funds in the United States if the European investment had not been made. Presumably the money would have been used for dividends or diversification, since ATC seemingly had ample funds for their U.S.

TABLE 6-10

U.S. EMPLOYMENT ESTIMATED TO EXIST IF AMERICAN TRACTOR
COMPANY HAD *NOT* UNDERTAKEN ITS 1965 EXPANSION IN
EUROPE, 1965–1970

(person-years)

Item	1965	1966	1967	1968	1969	1970
Merchandise Exports:[a]						
Tractors less than						
60 HP	0	270	306	324	344	344
Tractors 60 HP or						
greater	0	936	879	822	764	764
Merchandise Imports:						
Service	0	1	3	4	4	10
Total	0	1,207	1,188	1,150	1,112	1,118

[a] Includes materials and components as well as finished products.
NOTES:
Ratio of person-years to dollars of merchandise assumed to be the same as in
Table 6-9. Dollars of merchandise obtained from Table 6-7.

expansions in the tractor business. They continued to add
U.S. capacity throughout this period in order to meet their
U.S. requirements. Furthermore, as discussed in Chapter
1, U.S. fiscal and monetary policy swamp any U.S. investment effects of funds flow caused by foreign direct
investment.

Skill Level of U.S. Jobs

The net employment created in the United States during
the first six years of this investment contained a greater
share of professionals and skilled jobs than that existing in
U.S. manufacturing as a whole, 39 percent versus 34 percent, respectively. Table 6-12 shows these estimates.

* * * * *

This case illustrates the importance of two types of

TABLE 6-11

ESTIMATED *NET* CONTRIBUTION OF AMERICAN TRACTOR COMPANY'S
1965 EUROPEAN EXPANSION TO U.S. EMPLOYMENT, 1965–1970
(person-years)

Item	1965	1966	1967	1968	1969	1970
Merchandise Exports:[a]						
Tractors all sizes in anticipation of European expansion	2,467	0	0	0	0	0
Other tractors less than 60 HP	0	0	174	196	301	431
Other tractors 60 HP or greater	0	0	137	95	458	283
Equipment	739	0	0	0	0	0
Merchandise Imports:						
Service	0	0	0	0	0	0
Service Exports:						
Technology and management	40	40	40	40	40	40
Expatriates	22	22	22	22	22	22
Annual Total	3,268	62	373	353	821	776
Cumulative	3,268	3,330	3,703	4,056	4,877	5,653

[a] See note (a), Table 6-9.
SOURCE: Table 6-10 subtracted from Table 6-9.

exports that are often discussed by business executives in their arguments in favor of U.S. foreign direct investment: "anticipatory" exports made in order to build a foreign market prior to the start-up of foreign facilities and "associated" exports made as a result of the sales of the output of the foreign facilities. In this case, we estimate that these two categories of exports resulted in a net contribution to the U.S. balance of payments from 1965

TABLE 6-12

NET EFFECT OF AMERICAN TRACTOR COMPANY'S 1965 EXPANSION IN
EUROPE ON U.S. SKILL LEVELS FOR FIRST SIX YEARS OF PROJECT
COMPARED WITH AVERAGE OF ALL U.S. MANUFACTURING

| | Mix of job skills (percent) | |
	Created by European Expansion	Average for U.S. Manufacturing[a]
Professionals	17	15
Skilled	22	19
Clerical and Sales	17	16
Semi and Unskilled	44	50
Total	100	100
Two Highest Skill Levels[b]	39	34
Two Lowest Skill Levels	61	66

[a] Bureau of Labor Statistics, U.S. Department of Labor, *Tomorrow's Manpower Needs,* Vol. VI, Revised 1971, Bulletin 1737 (Washington, D. C.: U.S. Government Printing Office, 1972), pp. 33–35.
[b] Defined as "professionals" and "skilled."

through 1970 of $122 million, thereby far overshadowing both the financial flows and the types of exports more often recognized in analyses of the effects of U.S. foreign direct investment—that is, exports of equipment, materials, and components. However, our estimates of the "associated" exports probably are less accurate than our estimates of other categories of exports both in this and other chapters. For it is quite difficult to know with much degree of certainty the effects of a full, rather than a partial, product line on sales.

Another aspect of this case that seems a little unusual is the great divergence between balance-of-payments effects and employment effects. Although the balance-of-payments effects in sum are positive, the large outflows of loans cause the effects registered for some years to be negative. In contrast, the employment effects are positive in all years, because of the U.S. trade surplus created by the investment.

Finally—and this is a theme that recurs repeatedly throughout this book—some of the major competitors of the U.S. firms are large firms with international distribution systems rather than local firms selling only in local markets. In this case, Massey-Ferguson, a Canadian firm, not only has the largest output of any tractor company in the world, but its combined EEC and U.K. output is almost as large as that of all U.S. tractor companies put together (Table 6-5).

7

A Potpourri of
Other Cases

IN ADDITION TO THE FIVE CASES described earlier in detail, four other cases also have considerable interest for those studying (or making) foreign investments, and a summary of each is provided here. The purposes of three of these investments are similar to those in cases already fully treated.

Fabricated metals in Andina is an investment made to serve the local market in a less-developed country.

Paper in Canada is an investment made to serve the Canadian market.

Oil in Ireland is an investment made to serve European markets at low cost.

The remaining case, and the first one described in this chapter, appears on the surface to be similar to the two Canadian cases—an investment made in a developed country to serve the local market. But, in fact, the prohibitions of the host country against wholly owned foreign operations and its tight controls over imports have made this nation unique among the major industrial powers of the noncommunist world. The nation, of course, is Japan.

CHEMICALS IN JAPAN

A diversified U.S. chemical firm, with the disguised name of U.S. Chemical Company, formed a joint venture with a Japanese partner in 1961 to build a plant to manufacture low-density polyethylene (LDPE) in Japan primarily to serve the Japanese market. LDPE is used for many purposes, but mostly to make plastic films and sheets for packaging, coatings for a variety of items ranging from milk cartons to cables, and injection-molded housewares and toys.

U.S. Chemical invested $5 million in equity plus some technical know-how for a 50 percent interest in the joint venture. The high tariffs on LDPE in Japan, representing about one-third of the U.S. sales price for the product, effectively prevented the U.S. company from exporting from its U.S. plant to Japan. Differences in labor costs per unit of LDPE output, on the other hand, were quite small.

Few details are available on the inner workings of U.S. Chemical in this case. We obtained our information from a manager typical of the highly trained technocrats who populate giant multinational enterprises but who are not privy to the inner councils of the firm. However, we do know that the management of U.S. Chemical Company expected that the joint venture would earn 10 percent on its gross operating investment, which U.S. Chemical Company defined as net working capital plus fixed assets. In fact, the venture earned closer to 5 percent. Plant capacity was expanded in 1963 by "debottlenecking," but no new funds were required from the United States. In

1967, however, when substantially more capacity was needed, U.S. Chemical invested another $5.25 million, this time in the form of a loan. This new investment increased the flow of funds back to the United States. Immediate interest and principal payments began, and dividends were increased in accordance with an agreement between the two parent companies that half of the net income would be paid out as dividends.

We considered the two investments as one case, and our analysis starts with the conditions existing in 1961. If U.S. Chemical Company had not made the investment, and no other U.S. company had been allowed to invest, it seems very likely that the Japanese market would have been served either by the expansion of one of the six existing LDPE plants in Japan owned by non-U.S. firms, or, alternatively, by a new company formed with a partnership of a European firm and the Japanese firm that was U.S. Chemical's partner. In 1961 some nine non-U.S. firms had technology available for manufacturing low-density polyethylene, and three of these still had not made an investment in Japan to manufacture it.[1] If an existing non-U.S. firm in Japan had expanded, we estimate that the equipment (instrumentation) would not have been procured from the United States, for European LDPE manufacturers typically obtain such equipment from Europe.[2]

Although there were some exports of goods, principally equipment, the most important items affecting the balance of payments were the foreign direct investment items and the receipts of dividends and interest. As shown in Table 7-1, we estimate that the recoupment period for the U.S. balance of payments for the outflow of U.S. funds was some nine years. At first glance it appears that the injec-

---

[1] U.S. Chemical Company records.

[2] Interviews with several companies.

tion of fresh U.S. funds in 1967 made the recoupment period longer than it would otherwise have been. However, even without this expansion the recoupment period would have been about the same length of time; the second investment had a very short recoupment period because the U.S. loan was repaid within five years, and interest, larger dividends, and equipment exports took place in the meantime.

No person-years of work were lost in the United States because of the investment; hence, the recoupment period for lost jobs is zero. In fact, some jobs were created immediately in the United States because of the manufacture of the equipment (Table 7-2).

Relatively high skills are needed in the manufacture of equipment and in the provision of technical advice to foreign operations. Thus, the average skill levels in the employment created in the United States as a result of this investment were higher than those existing in the average of all U.S. manufacturing. The first and last columns of Table 7-3 show this. The two middle columns of Table 7-3 are used in the cases immediately following.

FABRICATED METALS IN ANDINA

The U.S. investor in this case is American Copper and Aluminum Company (AMCAL), the disguised name for a fully integrated U.S. producer of a wide range of copper and aluminum products. In 1968, AMCAL purchased a locally owned firm manufacturing wire and cable in a South American country which we call Andina. AMCAL made this purchase in order to gain a foothold in the Andina market, which was considered to be very attractive both because of its size and its expected growth. And the change perceived

TABLE 7-1

ESTIMATED *NET* EFFECTS OF U.S. CHEMICAL COMPANY'S 1961 INVESTMENT IN JAPAN ON U.S. BALANCE OF PAYMENTS, 1961–1972

(millions of dollars)

Line	Item	1961	1962	1963	1964	1965	1966	1967	1968	1969	1970[b]	1971	1972
	Estimated to be recorded with investment[a]												
	Merchandise Exports:												
1	Chemicals	0	.10	.05	.03	0	0	0	0	0	0	0	0
2	Equipment	1.80	0	0	0	0	0	1.30	0	0	0	0	0
	Service Exports:												
3	Management and technology	.12	.13	0	.05	0	0	.12	0	0	0	0	0
4	Dividends and interest	0	0	.30	.30	.34	.34	.49	.96	.96	.85	.73	.67
	Foreign Direct Investment:												
5	Equity	-3.00	-2.00	0	0	0	0	0	0	0	0	0	0
6	Loans	0	0	0	0	0	0	-5.25	1.05	1.05	1.05	1.05	1.05
7	Subtotals	-1.08	-1.77	.35	.38	.34	.34	-3.34	2.01	2.01	1.90	1.78	1.72

8 Estimated to be recorded if investment had not been made			0	0	0	0	0	0	0	0	0	0
9 Net effects of investment (Line 7 minus Line 8)	−1.08	−1.77	.35	.38	.34	.34	−3.34	2.01	2.01	1.90	1.78	1.72
10 Cumulative	−1.08	−2.85	−2.50	−2.12	−1.78	−1.44	−4.78	−2.77	−.76	1.14	2.92	4.64

a Based on actual experiences through 1970.

b Balance-of-payments outflow is recovered in 1970; recoupment period is nine years.

NOTES:

Estimated to be recorded with investment

Line 1: Only the polymerization catalysts and a few process chemicals were exported to the joint venture from the United States. U.S. Chemical Company personnel believe that since 1964 all such supplies have been purchased locally.

Line 2: U.S. Chemical Company estimated $1.3 million of the $15 million invested in 1967 consisted of capital equipment exported from the United States, largely instrumentation and laboratory equipment. Although such a detailed breakdown was lacking for the 1962 plant, we assume the proportion of U.S. equipment would be higher (10 percent instead of 8.7 percent) in earlier Japanese plants, given the recent progress of Japanese industrial instrumentation.

Line 3: Beyond the provision of a process design as equity contribution, U.S. Chemical Company provided the joint venture with an estimated ten person-years of engineering, start-up troubleshooting, management and marketing support during 1961–1962. In the absence of stated salaries, these employees are assumed to be charged at a cost, including full overhead, of $25,000 per person-year. A debottlenecking expansion in 1964 consisted of about two person-years at $25,000 each. The 1967 capacity was constructed and started and the products marketed with only nominal U.S. support, estimated at two person-years of engineering in the United States and two person-years of marketing assistance in Japan. These persons are assumed to be charged at $30,000 per person-year.

(Continued on next page.)

TABLE 7-1 (*continued*)

Line 5: Although U.S. Chemical Company expected to invest $5 million in cash in the joint venture and earn 10 percent return on gross operating investment (net income, divided by working capital plus fixed assets), the joint venture, operating in a competitive environment, has tended toward a 5 percent return as defined by U.S. Chemical. A contractual arrangement calls for 50 percent of net income to be paid as a dividend each year. The dividend repatriations to U.S. Chemical are based upon reconstructed balance sheets for 1961–1967 and the average performance for the period.

Line 6: About 35 percent of the financing for the second plant consisted of a U.S. bank loan of $5.25 million at half a percent over the prime rate. Repayment over five years from operating cash flows was estimated by U.S. Chemical personnel. All other financing was by Japanese banks and internally generated funds.

Estimated to be recorded if investment had not been made. In assessing the incremental effect of the investment, the "no investment" case was strongly influenced by the high probability that a similar low-density polyethylene plant would have been built by a competitor in the absence of U.S. Chemical's investment.

Chemicals: Catalysts and process chemicals, which were initially exported from the United States in the actual case, were readily available from the European LDPE producers and differed slightly for each process. No U.S. exports would have been expected if a U.S. company had not invested.

Equipment: We estimated that the presence of a non-U.S. chemical company (most probably European) as a venture partner would have eliminated the use of U.S. equipment in plant construction. Though 8 to 10 percent of fixed assets in the actual case were capital goods supplied from the United States, these would have been available from European equipment suppliers. A European process supplier would most probably have specified such sources based upon his prior experience. *Management and Technology*: With a European LDPE process and a Japanese prime contractor, no U.S. engineering services would be expected. In the same vein, marketing would be a joint European-Japanese function. No U.S. receipts for payment of engineering and marketing services or employment would be expected in the absence of a U.S. venture. *Foreign Direct Investment*: No U.S. equity or debt would be involved in a European-Japanese venture.

by foreign investors, including AMCAL, in Andina's political climate in the late 1960s made the market even more attractive. Tariffs on wire and cable were 55 percent and effectively limited imports.

AMCAL almost always had local partners but decided to start with a wholly owned operation in Andina in order to obtain freedom to expand the product line and output. AMCAL's international division planned to expand the local operations soon into high-technology projects, for they concluded that AMCAL had no important advantages over locally owned firms in the low-technology products, and the locally owned firms had lower overheads and paid less taxes on their profits than foreign investors typically did. For example, it was the common practice of local companies to understate billings in order to avoid tax liabilities; AMCAL calculated that the local company it acquired had understated sales and profits to the tax authorities by 30 percent.

But the plans of AMCAL's international division to expand in Andina soon after the acquisition were thwarted by a change of attitude toward international business on the part of the parent company's board of directors—apparently because of lower foreign profits than expected, a recession in the United States, and U.S. government controls on capital outflows. In 1969 the directors cancelled all approved capital requests over $20,000 for foreign investments and instructed the international division not to submit any requests for new projects unless they showed "substantial profit potential." In this atmosphere, AMCAL's international division decided to postpone its request for funds to expand the new acquisition in Andina.

But, by 1971, the international division's executives were forced to act. Competition had grown keener in Andina, thereby confirming the belief that AMCAL could

TABLE 7-2

ESTIMATED *NET* EFFECTS OF U.S. CHEMICAL COMPANY's 1961 INVESTMENT IN JAPAN
ON U.S. EMPLOYMENT, 1961–1972

(person-years)

Line	Item	1961	1962	1963	1964	1965	1966	1967	1968–1972
	Actuals recorded[a]								
	Merchandise Exports:								
1	Chemicals	0	2	1	1	0	0	0	0
2	Equipment	101	0	0	0	0	0	73	0
	Service Exports:								
3	Management and technology	5	5	0	2	0	0	4	0
4	Subtotals	106	7	1	3	0	0	77	0

5 Estimated to be recorded if investment had not taken place	0	0	0	0	0	0	0	0
6 Net effects of investment (Line 4 minus Line 5)	106	7	1	3	0	0	77	0
7 Cumulative	106	113	114	117	117	117	194	0

NOTES:

Estimated to be recorded with investment.

Line 1: Estimated on basis of $47,000 of output per employee (SIC 281, Industrial Chemicals; U.S. Department of Commerce, *Industrial Profiles*, October 1971, p. 111).

Line 2: Estimated on basis of 55.9 employees per million dollars of sales (SIC 3611, Electric Measuring Instruments; U.S. Bureau of the Census, *Census of Manufactures, 1967* [Washington, D.C.: Superintendent of Documents, 1971], Vol. 11, Industry Statistics, Part 3, p. 36A-16).

Line 3: Estimates by U.S. Chemical Company executives.

Estimated to be recorded if investment had not taken place: See Table 7-1 for explanations.

a Based on actual experience through 1970.

TABLE 7-3

Net Effect of Three U.S.-Owned Expansions Abroad on U.S.
Skill Levels for First Few Years[a] of Projects Compared
with Average for all U.S. Manufacturing

Mix of Job Skills (percent)

Job Skill Level	Chemicals in Japan	Metals in Andina	Paper in Canada	Average for U.S. Manufacturing[b]
Professionals	34	22	35	15
Skilled	11	22	21	19
Clerical and sales	14	18	11	16
Semiskilled and unskilled	41	38	33	50
Total	100	100	100	100
Two Highest Skill Levels[c]	45	44	56	34
Two Lowest Skill Levels	55	56	44	66

[a] The number of years of employment effects considered in the skill-level calculations are 12 for chemicals, 9 for metals, and 7 for paper.
[b] Bureau of Labor Statistics, U.S. Department of Labor, *Tomorrow's Manpower Needs*, Vol. IV, revised 1971, Bulletin 1737 (Washington, D.C.: Government Printing Office, 1972), pp. 33–35.
[c] Defined as "professionals" and "skilled."

operate profitably only if it manufactured relatively high-technology products. Furthermore, two other firms had decided to invest in Andina to manufacture high-technology products and AMCAL's executives feared that these firms would soon preempt the high-technology market. Thus, AMCAL's international executives faced a dilemma. Because they did not want to begin to report the worsening of the profit position that was anticipated if they did nothing, they faced two choices: sell out or expand. The board had sold three foreign subsidiaries since 1969; so the international division, not wanting to see more of their empire taken away, decided that the lesser of two evils was to request funds for expansion in Andina.

This was more than an ordinary request. The international executives viewed it as a test case to determine the likely future of international operations within AMCAL and, by implication, their personal futures. They prepared a sugar-coated package for the AMCAL board. AMCAL's existing operations would be combined with a $2-million equity investment by a European firm to form a 50-50 joint venture. Each parent would then make a long-term loan of $2 million, denominated in dollars and bearing an interest rate of 11 percent. An additional $4 million of short-term funds would be borrowed locally. This proposal had three advantages from the viewpoint of the board. It met their desire to have joint ventures rather than wholly owned operations; it removed a potential competitor from the scene; and the return of funds to the United States looked attractive. For not only would AMCAL earn 11 percent interest on the loan, it also would receive a fee for managing the subsidiary and would obtain a larger captive outlet for its exports of refined copper from its U.S. facilities. Even though the original owner had purchased raw materials from Europe, AMCAL now supplied them from its U.S. operations and was to continue this practice under its agreement with its proposed joint-venture partner. The board approved the project in 1971 for start-up in 1973.

What would have happened if neither AMCAL nor any other U.S. firm had been allowed to invest in Andina? In that case, we estimate that non-U.S. firms would have invested in Andina to an amount sufficient to meet Andina's desire not to import large quantities of wire and cable. Although there were numerous locally owned firms manufacturing wire and cable in Andina in 1968, none were manufacturing high-technology products. But all of the five foreign-owned firms did, and two of these were non-U.S. owned. Of the two additional foreign firms that had decided by 1971 to begin manufacturing high-technology products, one was non-U.S. owned. In addition to these three non-U.S. firms that had entered Andina by the early 1970's, there existed an additional eight non-U.S. firms, each of whom had at least three foreign investments in high-technology wire and cable manufacture elsewhere. We judge that these firms, in conjunction with the non-U.S. foreign investors already in Andina, would have had no problem in manufacturing Andina's wire and cable needs in Andina. Further, if non-U.S. firms had expanded in place of U.S. firms, we estimate that they would have obtained their imported equipment from their home country, or in the case of a European firm, either from its home country or a neighboring country. Our interviews revealed that prices for equipment are comparable in the United States and Europe, and the proximity of the parent's home office to equipment suppliers and its experience in working with these suppliers would be the major determinant of which country would supply the equipment.

Our analysis of the effects of AMCAL's investments in 1968 and 1973 on the U.S. balance of payments shows a recoupment period of the original capital outflow of some six years (Table 7-4). The largest positive flows are from the equipment exports. The next most important are the exports of raw materials and the receipts of interest and dividends. The expansion of 1973 reduces the recoupment period, for it results in equipment exports that exceed the new capital outflow as well as increases in exports of raw materials and receipts of interest.

The employment effects on the United States were positive from the time of the initial investment, which caused no displacement of U.S. labor—primarily, of course, because no U.S. exports were displaced as a result of the investment (Table 7-5).

As might be expected with the relatively large exports of equipment, the skill level of the jobs created in the United States as a result of investments in Andina was higher than the skill levels existing on the average for all U.S. manufacturing (as Table 7-3 illustrates).

Paper in Canada

Kimberly-Clark,[3] a Wisconsin-based corporation, made its first investment in Canada in 1920 in order to assure a supply of pulp for its paper mill at Niagara Falls, New York. Kimberly-Clark continued to expand in foreign countries and by 1970 its total assets in wholly owned subsidiaries in Canada approximated $70 million, in addition to part interests in two other pulp and paper companies.

Since 1964, Kimberly-Clark-Canada (KCC) had been short of capacity for making paper wadding, an intermediate product used to make sanitary paper products, such as facial tissues, household towels, and table napkins. KCC made up this deficit by purchasing wadding from other Canadian manufacturers, all of whom were converting wadding into final products competitive with KCC's. KCC considered it risky to rely on competitors indefinitely for a key intermediate product. Quality was not assured nor easily controlled, supply was subject to the marketing plans of the competitors, and prices fluctuated widely, as much as 16 percent for the same product delivered to the same location at the same time. In spite of these wide fluctuations, the lowest prices from Canadian

---

[3] Because the name of the firm in this case is not disguised, certain facts have been changed for competitive reasons, but the conclusions of our analysis have not been affected.

TABLE 74

Estimated *Net* Effects of AMCAL's 1968 Investment in Andina on U.S. Balance of Payments, 1968–1976

(*millions of dollars*)

Line	Item	1968	1969	1970	1971	1972	1973	1974[b]	1975	1976
	Estimated to be recorded with investment[a]									
	Merchandise Exports:									
1	Raw materials	0	.04	.09	.11	.11	.14	.18	.27	.35
2	Products not made in Andina	0	.01	.01	.01	.01	.01	.01	.01	.01
3	Equipment	0	.24	0	0	0	2.50	0	0	0
	Service Exports:									
4	Technical fees	0	0	0	0	0	.10	.10	.15	.19
5	Dividends and interest	0	0	.01	.01	.01	.22	.22	.22	.18
	Foreign Direct Investment:									
6	Equity	−2.00	0	0	0	0	0	0	0	0
7	Loans	0	0	0	0	0	−2.00	0	0	.40
8	Subtotals	−2.00	.29	.11	.13	.13	.97	.51	.65	1.13

Estimated to be recorded if investment had not been made

Merchandise Exports:

9 Products made in Andina	0	0	0	0	0	.01	.01	.01	.01
10 Net effects of investment (Line 8 minus Line 9)	−2.00	.29	.11	.13	.13	.96	.50	.64	1.12
11 Cumulative	−2.00	−1.71	−1.60	−1.47	−1.34	−.38	.12	.76	1.88

[a] Actual data available through first eight months of 1971.

[b] Balance-of-payments outflow is recovered in 1974; recoupment period is six years.

SOURCE: Company estimates.

TABLE 7-5

Estimated *NET* Effects of AMCAL's 1968 Investment in Andina on U.S. Employment, 1968–1976

(person-years)

Line	Item	1968	1969	1970	1971	1972	1973	1974	1975	1976
	Estimated to be recorded with investment[a]									
	Merchandise Exports:									
1	Raw materials	0	0	1	1	1	1	1	2	2
2	Products not made in Andina	0	0	0	0	1	0	0	0	0
3	Equipment	0	9	0	0	0	96	0	0	0
	Service Exports:									
4	Technical and management assistance	3	3	4	5	5	5	5	5	5
5	Subtotals	3	12	5	6	7	102	6	7	7

Estimated to be recorded if
investment had not been made

Merchandise Exports:

6 Products made in Andina	0	0	0	0	0	0	0	1
7 Net effects of investment (Line 5 minus Line 6)	3	12	5	6	7	102	6	7	6
8 Cumulative	3	15	20	26	33	135	141	148	154

a Actual data available through first eight months of 1971.

NOTES:

Line 1: These raw materials are refined copper. We estimated 6.84 employees per million dollars of sales for 1964, from SIC 3331, "primary copper," in U.S. Department of Commerce, *Industry Profiles, 1958–1969*, p. 163. This overstates employment to the extent that the input to the refining process is imported, and the United States is a net importer of copper ore and blister from which refined copper is made. However, our estimates of employment effects are so small we did not refine them further.

Lines 2 and 6: 13.6 employees per million dollars of sales for 1969, from SIC 3351, "copper rolling and drawing," *ibid.*, p. 167. Only one person-year was used for line 2 and one for line 6 during all years. This one person-year was shown by us in the first year in which the fractions of cumulative person-years exceed 0.5.

Line 3: 38.5 employees per million dollars of sales for 1969, from average of SIC 3542, "machine tools, metal-forming types," *ibid.*, p. 198 and SIC 3548, "metal working machinery, nec," *ibid.*, p. 199.

Line 4: Expatriates average one person a year from 1968–1976. Headquarters staff (managers, accountants, clerks, and secretaries) averaged two persons yearly through 1970 and three persons yearly from 1971 onward. Technical assistance averages one person yearly from 1970–1976. SOURCE: Company records.

competitors were still substantially higher than KCC's manufacturing costs for the same product.

It was possible for KCC to obtain wadding from Kimberly-Clark's U.S. operations, but since the Kimberly-Clark parent organization attempted to operate all subsidiaries as independent profit centers, prices on sales from Kimberly-Clark-U.S. to Kimberly-Clark-Canada were set on an arm's-length basis. It was standard practice for Kimberly-Clark-U.S. to offer to supply Kimberly-Clark-Canada at total costs plus 13.3 percent, up to the quantity available from U.S. excess capacity. To this was added transportation and a 17.5 percent duty, which resulted in a higher price to Kimberly-Clark-Canada than they could obtain from local competitors.[4] Hence, KCC seldom purchased wadding from the United States (although from time to time KCC did obtain new products from the United States for market tests and market development prior to manufacturing the products in Canada.) But even if KCC had wanted to do so, Kimberly-Clark-U.S. was not a steady supplier, for it often was short of wadding and made purchases from other U.S. firms, and such was the case in 1968 when KCC management decided that a new Canadian wadding mill was needed.

KCC management prepared a request for the project and presented it to the parent in March 1969. The estimated profitability was an internal rate of return of 12 percent annually on a total project outlay of $20 million; but perhaps more important than any estimated return on investment, the president of Kimberly-Clark-Canada told

---

[4] One might have expected a corporation of the size and experience of Kimberly-Clark (in 1970 foreign sales of $300 million out of total sales of $850 million, and over 50 years of foreign experience) to have operated more as a "profit maximizer" rather than use so rigidly such rules of thumb; see Sidney M. Robbins and Robert B. Stobaugh, *Money in the Multinational Enterprise: A Study in Financial Policy* (New York: Basic Books, 1973), Chapter 3.

the parent's executives: "In our view, it is necessary, in order to maintain a progressive and viable business, unhampered by restrictions of tonnage, that this project be approved; only by having this flexibility will we be able to preserve or improve our position in the market."[5]

In line with KCC's tradition of being a semiautonomous entity and relying on its own sources of funds for its capital needs, the parent provided no new equity funds. The parent did, however, lend KCC $5.1 million of idle funds in 1971 for repayment the following year. This loan, as well as loans from the two Canadian corporations owned partially by Kimberly-Clark-U.S., carried interest rates equivalent to those of commercial banks and in effect represented investment opportunities for the lender in addition to a source of funds for the borrower. For KCC had a $15.7 million credit line from Canadian banks, which, when combined with a $4 million grant from the Canadian government and some retained earnings, provided more than the $20 million needed for the project.

The project was approved in 1969 and the new mill started operation in March 1971. The 1970 Canadian recession caused Canadian sales of sanitary paper products to be lower than KCC had projected for 1971. This was taken into account in our estimates for the subsequent years of the project.

We estimate that if Kimberly-Clark had not expanded in 1970, a non-U.S. firm would have provided the new capacity for the wadding, though perhaps not until 1974, for excess capacity as a whole existed in the Canadian industry. In 1971 two Canadian-owned firms—E. B. Eddy and Perkins Paper—were capable of adding a new mill. These two firms had broad product lines, though not identical with KCC's. In addition to the two Canadian firms, at

---
[5] Company records.

least two large European paper companies, each with total sales in excess of $500 million and with substantially larger sales outside the United States than any U.S. paper company except International Paper, very likely could have provided any new capacity needed in Canada.[6]

The 17.5 percent Canadian tariff and added freight costs make it unprofitable for U.S. firms to build capacity in the United States for the Canadian market. For example, U.S. products without any U.S. profit would cost KCC some 25 percent more than the cost of producing its Canadian goods with a typical KCC profit margin before tax of 8 to 10 percent. Of course, some Canadians would be willing to buy the American brand-name products even if the products were imported from the United States and sold for high prices. In view of the lack of data and in the belief that the magnitudes are low, we ignored this possibility in our analysis. To the extent these U.S. exports would exist, our analysis overstates the benefits of the KCC investment to the U.S. economy.

Our analysis shows that the effects of the investment on the U.S. balance of payments are positive, primarily because of the export of some $1.6 million in U.S. equipment (Table 7-6). A large outflow of U.S. funds took place because of the parent company's loan in 1971, but this is estimated to have been reversed in 1972 when the loan was scheduled to be repaid; thus the recoupment period is two years after the start of the project but only one year after the initial outflow of funds. The cumulative effect on the U.S. balance of payments remains positive for all subsequent years.

We estimate that the investment created a net total of 69 person-years of employment in the United States in the first year, 1970, primarily because of equipment exports,

---

[6] Robert B. Stobaugh, et al., *The Likely Effects on the U.S. Economy of Eliminating the Deferral of U.S. Income Tax on Foreign Earnings,* p. 51.

so the recoupment period is zero (Table 7-7). These 69 person-years are partially offset in 1974, the year in which we estimate that some U.S. exports of equipment would have occurred if KCC's investment had not been made. But overall we estimate the net effect on U.S. employment for 1970 through 1976 to be a positive 62 person-years of employment. And these jobs contain substantially higher job skills than the average for all U.S. manufacturing, as Table 7-3 points out.

OIL IN IRELAND

In 1966, Gulf Oil Corporation decided that one of its wholly owned foreign subsidiaries would construct a $30-million facility in Ireland to accommodate supertankers bringing oil from Kuwait. The oil would be loaded onto smaller tankers for shipment to European ports that could not handle supertankers. But this $30 million was only the tip of the iceberg, for an additional $165 million of U.S. funds was needed—$15 million by Gulf for its one-half share of the expansion of the Kuwait terminal (British Petroleum owned the other half) and $150 million by National Bulk Carriers, Inc., for six 326,000-ton tankers (made in Japan) that were to be chartered to Gulf on a long-term basis for use on the Kuwait-to-Ireland run. Gulf made the investment and chartered the tankers to provide the facilities needed to transport increasing quantities of Kuwait crude oil at low cost.

We estimate that if Gulf Oil had not made this investment, exports of crude oil from the United States would not have been increased to serve the European markets. Although the United States was a major oil exporter early in the life cycle of the industry, crude oil prices by the 1960s were substantially higher in the United States than

TABLE 7-6

Estimated *Net* Effects of Kimberly-Clark's 1971 Investment in Canada on U.S. Balance of Payments, 1970–1976

(millions of dollars)

Line	Item	1970	1971	1972[a]	1973	1974	1975	1976
	Estimated to be recorded with investment							
	Merchandise Exports:							
1	Equipment	1.61	0	0	0	0	0	0
2	Raw materials for products not made in expansion	0	0	.01	.02	.03	.04	.05
	Service Exports:							
3	Management and technical fees	.32	0	0	0	0	0	0
4	Royalties	0	.03	.09	.23	.31	.38	.45
5	Dividends and interest	0	.26	.07	0	0	0	0
	Foreign Direct Investment:							
6	Equity	0	0	0	0	0	0	0
7	Loans	0	−5.10	5.10	0	0	0	0
8	Subtotals	1.93	−4.81	5.27	.25	.34	.42	.50

Estimated to be recorded if investment had not been made

Merchandise Exports:

9 Equipment	0	0	0	0	.50	0	0
Service Exports:							
10 Management and technical fees	0	0	0	0	.18	0	0
11 Dividends and interest	0	0	.52	.53	.39	.31	.31
12 Subtotals	0	0	.52	.53	1.07	.31	.31
13 Net effects of investment (Line 8 minus Line 12)	1.93	-5.33	4.74	-.14	-.73	.11	.19
14 Cumulative	1.93	-3.40	1.34	1.20	.47	.58	.77

a Balance-of-payments outflow is recovered in 1972; recoupment period is two years.

NOTES:

Estimated to be recorded with investment

Line 1: Total equipment purchases were $13.8 million, of which $365,000 was assembled equipment purchased directly from U.S. suppliers; $172,000 was unassembled equipment purchased directly from U.S. suppliers for assembly in Canada; $574,000 was the U.S. component of the equipment purchased from the principal Canadian supplier, Beloit, a subsidiary of a U.S. equipment manufacturer. No information was available on the source of the remaining $12.7 million; we estimated that $0.5 million represented equipment and associated materials from the United States.

Line 2: We accepted Kimberly-Clark's estimates that failure to expand in sanitary paper napkins would adversely affect its market position in feminine napkins, the raw materials for which were obtained from the United States. The estimates here reflect the following losses in U.S. exports of these materials, compared with what they would otherwise be—none in 1971, increasing 1 percent yearly until the loss reached 5 percent in 1976.

Line 3: U.S. services, rendered mostly by engineers of Kimberly-Clark-U.S. and Beloit-U.S., during construction and start-up of plant.

Line 4: Incremental royalties generated by the increased sales that resulted from the expansion.

(*Continued on next page.*)

TABLE 7-6 *(continued)*

Line 5: Interest on the $5.1 million loan made by the parent to the Canadian subsidiary in 1971. A $425,000 dividend remitted in early 1971 was omitted by us from both line 5 and line 11, since it was paid from earnings made prior to the 1971 expansion and was not affected by the investment. Our estimates do not include income received by Beloit for its Canadian subsidiaries' approximately $5 million of sales of equipment to Kimberly-Clark-Canada.

Remittances of dividends are expected to jump sharply from KCC after 1976 when the bank loan is paid off; cash flow will increase by $3 million annually.

Line 6: No new equity investment was made, for the $20-million expansion was financed entirely from earnings, borrowed funds, and a $4-million grant from the Area Development Agency of the federal government.

Line 7: A loan of $5.1 million was made from the parent to the subsidiary in 1971 from idle funds held by the parent, but in 1972 the subsidiary increased its local bank borrowings to repay the parent. This repayment was in accordance with Kimberly-Clark-Canada's tradition of having become a semiautonomous entity relying on its own sources of funds for its capital needs ever since a 1957 reorganization.

Estimated to be recorded if investment had not been made

Line 9: If a Canadian firm had expanded, we estimate that a greater share of the equipment would have come from Canada and the United Kingdom, thereby resulting in lower U.S. exports than was the case with the expansion. Furthermore, although Kimberly-Clark was short on capacity in Canada, excess capacity existed within the industry, so it is likely that another firm would not have expanded until 1974.

Line 10: This would have been lower than in the "investment case" because of fewer purchases of U.S. equipment.

Line 11: These would have been higher than under the "no investment" case because part of the earnings from the existing plant would have been paid as dividends instead of reinvested (we made estimates of payout from historical averages).

abroad and U.S. firms could not serve their European markets from the United States. On the other hand, because of the stringent U.S. system of oil import quotas, investment abroad could not increase U.S. imports. If Gulf had not made this investment and no U.S. competitor had been allowed to expand production to serve the market, foreign competitors—European multinational enterprises, domestic European firms, and companies owned by oil-producing nations—would have expanded to do so.

The United States could not compete with foreign competitors in the construction of tankers, and, indeed, had no shipyard capable of building supertankers. In fact, in the late 1960s only four shipyards in the world could build ships larger than 300,000 tons, and two of these were in Japan. Neither were U.S. firms competitive in terms of cost in the export of equipment and materials for the terminals. In this case, for instance, virtually all of the terminal facilities were made with non-U.S. equipment, materials, and labor, although several of the contractors were foreign subsidiaries of U.S. firms.

In our analysis of the effects of this investment on the U.S. balance of payments, we assume that the entire $195 million came from the United States, even though some of the funds could be construed as coming from Europe, for they were drawn from Gulf's worldwide pool of funds that included Eurodollar loans. The outflows of $195 million over five years were offset by Gulf's profits from increased oil sales. These profits resulted in a recoupment period of six years (Table 7-8). We ignored any profit remittances by U.S. contractors involved in building the terminal facilities.

We estimate the employment effects as zero. True, some of the staff in Gulf's Pittsburgh headquarters undoubtedly spent some working time on the expansion, but

TABLE 7-7

ESTIMATED *NET* EFFECTS OF KIMBERLY-CLARK'S 1971 INVESTMENT IN CANADA ON
U.S. EMPLOYMENT, 1970–1976

(person-years)

Line	Item	1970	1971	1972	1973	1974	1975	1976
	Estimated to be recorded with investment							
	Merchandise Exports:							
1	Equipment	56	0	0	0	0	0	0
2	Raw materials for products not made in expansion	0	0	0	0	0	1	1
	Service Exports:							
3	Management and technical	13	0	0	0	0	0	0
4	Royalties	0	0	1	2	3	4	5
5	Subtotals	69	0	1	2	3	5	6

Estimated if investment had not been made							
Merchandise Exports:							
6 Equipment	0	0	0	0	17	0	0
Service Exports:							
7 Management and technical	0	0	0	0	7	0	0
8 Subtotals	0	0	0	0	24	0	0
9 Net effects of investment (Line 5 minus Line 8)	69	0	1	2	-21	5	6
10 Cumulative	69	69	70	72	51	56	62

NOTES:

Lines 1 and 6: 34.9 employees per million dollars of shipments for SIC 3554, "paper industries machinery," from U.S. Department of Commerce, *Industry Profiles*, 1958–1969 (Washington: Superintendent of Documents, October 1971), p. 202, for 1969.

Line 2: 15.7 employees per million dollars of shipments for SIC 2647, "sanitary paper products," from *ibid.*, p. 96, for 1969.

Lines 3 and 7: Estimated on basis of $25,000 per person-year.

Line 4: We do not know the effect of royalties received from foreign subsidiaries on U.S. research and development activities. For lack of better information, we estimate that each $100,000 annually of royalty income represents one person-year of employment.

TABLE 7-8

ESTIMATED *NET* EFFECTS ON GULF OIL'S 1966 INVESTMENT IN IRELAND ON U.S.
BALANCE OF PAYMENTS, 1966–1972

(millions of dollars)

Line Item	1966	1967	1968	1969	1970	1971	1972 [b]
Estimated to be recorded with investment[a]							
Service Exports:							
1 Dividends and interest	0	0	48	48	48	48	48
Foreign Direct Investment:							
2 Gulf Oil	−15	−15	−15	0	0	0	0
3 National Bulk Carriers	−30	−30	−30	−30	−30	0	0
4 Subtotal	−45	−45	3	18	18	48	48

5 Estimated to be recorded if investment had not been made	0	0	0	0	0	0
6 Net effects of investment (Line 4 minus Line 5)	-45	-45	3	18	18	48
7 Cumulative	-45	-90	-87	-69	-51	-3

[a] Actuals for 1966–1970.

[b] Balance-of-payments outflow is recovered in 1972; recoupment period is six years.

NOTES:

Line 1: Estimated earnings from sale of approximately 80 million barrels per year delivered to Europe by six 326,000-ton tankers. This assumes an average load of 310,000 tons, 36 annual trips, and $.60 average net earnings per barrel for first five years of twenty-year charter. This approach is reinforced by the fact that the vast majority of Gulf's earnings are branch earnings, which are automatically included as inflows in balance-of-payments accounting. (Although not shown in table, we expected lower earnings in subsequent 15 years as competitive advantage of Gulf's supertankers declined with the increasing use of supertankers by others.)

Line 2: Ireland investment ($30 million) plus Gulf's 50 percent share of Kuwait terminal investment ($15 million) spread over the construction period.

Line 3: National Bulk's $150 million tanker investment period spread over five years.

even approximate numbers are difficult to judge. There-fore, our estimates understate the positive effects of the investment on the U.S. economy.

However, this is a narrow view of the outcome and does not represent the long-run alternative cost of not making the investment, which would have meant that Gulf would lose its crude oil supply from its entire Middle Eastern properties if it failed to make investments aimed at increas-ing tanker capacity and staying competitive. The loss would amount to over $4 billion over the life of the investment.[7]

In fact, if no American oil companies were allowed to expand overseas, they would lose income from all of their international operations, because the companies could no longer fulfill their function of providing large outlets for the oil-producing countries and large supplies for the consum-ers.[8] They would be replaced by a combination of European multinational enterprises, operating companies of national oil companies from the producing countries, and oil com-panies domiciled in the major consuming countries. Yet this would take some time, for although the U.S. firms were losing ground, they produced over half of the world's oil in 1973. How long it would take to replace the U.S. firms is difficult to estimate, for, as *Time* magazine quoted Colonel Qaddafi as replying in 1973 when asked why he did not throw the Americans out of Libya, "Nothing would please me more but who else would pump the oil that we need? God damn America."[9]

---

[7] Estimated by us from data in U.S. Department of Commerce, *U.S. Direct Investments Abroad, 1966, Part 1: Balance of Payments Data* (Washington: Superintendent of Documents, 1970), p. 95, considering Gulf's Middle Eastern holdings.

[8] For example, Exxon still planned a high level of capital expenditures in Venezuela even though it expected a takeover of its properties by the Venezuelan government, *Wall Street Journal*, January 10, 1975, p. 17.

[9] *Time*, April 2, 1973, p. 26.

8

What the Nine Cases Show

In dealing with capitalism we are dealing with an evolutionary process.[1]

JOSEPH SCHUMPETER'S REMARK has wider application than he had reason to believe. Written with very little reference to international business, his description of the capitalistic process is especially appropriate in describing our nine cases. Rather than taking bold leaps forward into new situations that promised high returns, the managers in our firms took small steps that represented a low-risk route in the normal course of their firm's evolution. They resembled Caspar Milquetoast more than Sir Francis Drake.

In most instances, the company managers were pushed into the decision to invest by some external pressure, usually associated with holding or maintaining a long-term position in an oligopolistic market structure. In one case,

---

[1] Joseph A. Schumpeter, "Capitalism and Creative Destruction," in Edwin Mansfield (ed.), *Monopoly Power and Economic Performance* (New York: W. W. Norton, 1968), p. 27; originally appeared in *Capitalism, Socialism and Democracy* (New York: Harper & Row, 1942).

Michigan Motors in Asiana, the firm was already losing its share of the market before it invested. But more often the purpose was to maintain the firm's position in a given product line within the local market as that market grew—the expansions in paper and tires in Canada and chemicals in Japan are examples. And sometimes the investment in a host country was made primarily to maintain a market in some *other* country, for example, the food plant in East Africa, the electronics plant in Taiwan, and the oil facility in Ireland. And in one case, tractors in Europe, the investment was made to maintain the firm's place in a worldwide oligopoly.

In only two of the cases did the managers reach out to obtain business in a new market. In one case, chemicals in Japan, the initial investment was made primarily in the hope of reaping dividends. In the other case, the initial acquisition of a metals plant in Andina was made as much to buy information about Andina as it was to earn the profits from the acquisition. Also in this case the firm feared that competitors would preempt the market for high-technology products.

Because the Hufbauer-Adler model[2] shows that investment abroad is favorable to the United States in those cases in which the U.S. firms are forced to produce abroad to serve the foreign markets, it is not surprising that the results of the investments which we studied are favorable on the average to the U.S. economy. For in most of our cases, competitive pressures forced the managers to invest abroad in order to serve the market serviced by the foreign plant in the case.

---

[2] The reader will recall from Chapter 1 that this is the best analytical model now available to indicate the effects of U.S. foreign direct investment on the U.S. balance of payments; see Hufbauer and Adler, *Overseas Manufacturing Investments and the Balance of Payments* (Washington, D.C.: U.S. Treasury Department, 1968), pp. 67–68.

For our nine cases, we estimated that the average recoupment period for the U.S. balance of payments, measured by the simple arithmetic mean, was 5.3 years, with a range of zero to 16 years. That is, on the average it took 5.3 years for the cumulative stream of balance-of-payments inflows caused by the investment to offset the balance-of-payments outflows caused by the investment.

Our estimates of employment effects are even more favorable for the U.S. economy, with an average recoupment period of 3.0 years and a range of zero to 22 years. It is only natural that the employment effects would be more favorable than the balance-of-payments effects, because some of the negative balance-of-payments effects are represented by an outflow of funds that do not have a negative employment effect. For reasons given in Chapter 1, we omitted any consideration of what the alternative use of funds in the United States might have been if the investment had not been made.

The recoupment periods just discussed were obtained by the use of our most likely estimate for each item that affected the recoupment period. We refer to such recoupment periods as the "most likely" results. However, because our estimates of the effects of the investments contained, by necessity, a good bit of judgment, we prepared a sensitivity analysis for each investment. In each analysis the individual item with the largest impact was assumed to be double our most likely estimate of this item and then half of our most likely estimate. In some cases these individual items were time periods, such as the period that we estimated would be needed for foreign-owned production to replace U.S. exports if the investment had not been made. Thus, in such an instance, a doubling of the time period would cause the investment to have a longer recoupment period than the one calculated with our most likely estimate of the time period. In other cases the individual item with the largest impact was U.S. exports, such as U.S. exports of equipment. In such a case, a doubling of our most likely estimate of U.S. exports would result in a recoupment period shorter than the one calculated with our most likely estimate.

In place of the 5.3 years as the average recoupment period for the balance-of-payments effects for our "most likely" results, the arithmetic average of the shortest recoupment periods becomes 3.0 years, and the longest 8.4 years. And instead of our most likely estimate of 3.0 years as the average recoupment period for the employment effects, the arithmetic average of the shortest recoupment period becomes 1.4 years and the longest 6.1 years. Table 8-1 presents the estimates for each of the nine cases.

These results are more favorable for the U.S. balance of payments than those indicated by Hufbauer and Adler's analysis—in fact, the arithmetic average of our longest estimates of recoupment periods (8.4 years) for the balance of payments is about the same as their estimate of 8.1 to 9.2 years under their most favorable assumed conditions.[3]

To be sure, no definite conclusions can be reached from nine cases whose representativeness cannot be tested. But we cannot resist the temptation to analyze the results. For without such pleasures, we would agree with Charles Darwin's anguished cry: "I begin to think that everyone who publishes a book is a fool."[4]

In any case, the reasons for the differences between the results of our cases and the Hufbauer-Adler model are of

---

[3] Hufbauer and Adler, ibid., pp. 67–68.

[4] Charles Darwin, in letter to Sir Joseph Dalton Hooker, February 1875, as quoted in Francis Darwin (ed.), *The Life and Letters of Charles Darwin* (London: J. Murray, 1887).

interest to persons who wish to study this subject further. Thus, we take the rest of this chapter to compare in detail our results with those of Hufbauer and Adler. This comparison, of course, is limited to balance of payments, since Hufbauer and Adler did not make employment estimates.

FINANCIAL FLOWS RESULTING FROM TRADE EFFECTS

As discussed in Chapter 1, the trade effects are the most important items in an analysis of the effects of U.S. foreign direct investment on the U.S. balance of payments, and assumptions about the investment behavior of firms are needed in order to estimate these trade effects. Eight different sets of assumptions regarding investment behavior are possible, each set comprising one of two possible outcomes for each of three possible situations:[5]

(1) U.S. firm which invested abroad could have exported from the United States instead of investing abroad (yes or no).

(2) Aggregate investment in the United States is reduced as a result of the U.S. firm's foreign investment (yes or no).

(3) Aggregate investment in host country is increased as a result of U.S. firm's foreign investment (yes or no).

Hufbauer and Adler worked principally with two of the sets of assumptions:[6]

(1) The U.S. firm which invested abroad could have exported (or have continued to export) from the United States instead of investing abroad, but instead chose to invest abroad. Its foreign investment reduces investment in the United States and increases investment in the host

---

[5] Possible sets, where Y = yes and N = no, are Y–Y–Y, Y–Y–N, Y–N–Y, Y–N–N, N–Y–Y, N–Y–N, N–N–Y and N–N–N.

[6] Hufbauer and Adler, *Overseas Manufacturing Investment*, p. 6.

TABLE 8-1

Sensitivity Analyses of Effects on the U.S. Balance of Payments and U.S. Employment of Nine Selected U.S. Foreign Direct Investments

| | | | Estimates of recoupment periods (years) | | | | | |
| | | | Balance of payments | | | Employment | | |
Chapter	Case	Individual item with largest impact	Most likely	If individual item with largest impact is doubled	If individual item with largest impact is halved	Most likely	If individual item with largest impact is doubled	If individual item with largest impact is halved
2	Michigan Motors—Asiana	Five years needed for foreign-owned output to replace $3.2 million of Michigan Motors' U.S. exports of unassembled vehicles to Asiana if foreign-owned firms had expanded in Asiana instead of Michigan Motors.	3	4	2	0	0	0
3	Intertire—Canada	Six years needed for foreign-owned output to replace Intertire's U.S. exports of tires to Canada if foreign firms had added capacity in Canada instead of Intertire.	16	28	7	22	45	11

4	Level of royalties received by American Food Processors as a result of payments by its East African affiliate.	3	2	4	(Not applicable because there are no effects on U.S. employment)		
American Food Processors—East Africa							
5	Five years needed for foreign-owned production to replace Systek's U.S. production if Systek had not built Taiwan plant.	4	10	2	5	10	2
Systek—Taiwan							
6	Level of American Tractor Company's exports in anticipation of starting of European plant.	0	0	2	0	0	0
American Tractor Company—Europe							
7	Net effect of U.S. Chemical's investment on U.S. exports of equipment to manufacture low-density polyethylene in Japan.	9	4	10	0	0	0
U.S. Chemical—Japan							
7	Net effect of AMCAL's investment on U.S. exports of equipment to manufacture cable and wire in Andina.	6	5	8	0	0	0
AMCAL—Andina							
7	Net effect of Kimberly-Clark's investment on U.S. exports of equipment to manufacture paper products in Canada.	2	2	2	0	0	0
Kimberly-Clark—Canada							
7	Gulf's investment reduced its operating cost by 60 cents a barrel.	6	3	10	(Not applicable because there are no effects on U.S. employment)		
Gulf Oil—Ireland							

country. Hufbauer and Adler refer to this as reducing investment in the United States and supplementing host-country investment. They call this set of assumptions the *classical* assumptions. (Note that this set is the equivalent of a "yes" to each of the three questions listed above.)

(2) The U.S. firm which invested abroad could not have exported (or have continued to export) from the United States. Its foreign investment does not reduce investment in the United States, because the U.S. firm would not have invested at all if it had not made the foreign investment. Nor does it increase investment in the host country, because a non-U.S. firm would have made the investment if the U.S. firm did not, They call this set of assumptions the *reverse classical* assumptions. (Note that this set is the equivalent of a "no" to each of the three questions listed above.)

Hufbauer and Adler also analyzed another set of assumptions, which they call *anticlassical*. These assumptions are similar to the classical set except that U.S. foreign direct investment supplements U.S. investment as well as foreign investment (note that this set is the equivalent of a "yes" to question numbers 1 and 3 above and a "no" to question number 2). The anticlassical assumption yields results very similar to those obtained with the classical assumptions. In the remainder of this chapter, we refer only to the classical and reverse classical assumptions.

Table 8-2 shows that under the classical assumptions, Hufbauer and Adler estimate fairly long recoupment periods for the U.S. balance of payments, and in most cases infinitely long; that is, the initial outflow is never recouped.[7] In contrast, their estimates of recoupment

---

[7] Hufbauer and Adler's initial estimates of recoupment periods were at such variance with the then currently accepted notions that they adjusted them downward in a number of cases. Their initial estimates are the maximum estimates shown

TABLE 8-2
MINIMUM AND MAXIMUM RECOUPMENT PERIODS
ESTIMATED BY HUFBAUER AND ADLER
(years)

Location of investment	*Classical assumptions*	*Reverse classical assumptions*
Canada	infinity	10.2
Latin America	infinity	9.8
Europe	7.5–18.8	6.5
Rest of world	22.2–infinity	6.7–infinity
World average[a]	infinity	8.1–9.2

[a] Based on amount of investment in each region.
SOURCE: G. C. Hufbauer and F. M. Adler, *Overseas Manufacturing Investments and the Balance of Payments* (Washington, D.C.: U.S. Treasury Department, 1968), pp. 67–68.

periods under the reverse classical assumptions range mostly from six to ten years with an average of somewhere around eight and a half years.

Which set of assumptions is more appropriate? Hufbauer and Adler hypothesize that "in the industrial countries, the initial period of classical substitution behavior should thus give way to reverse classical behavior within a few years [after the investment has been made]. In the underdeveloped countries, on the other hand, it may take a long time for reverse classical behavior to emerge."[8]

and their adjusted estimates are the minimum estimates shown in Table 8-2 (e.g., for investment in Europe under classical assumptions, the minimum is 7.5 and the maximum is 18.8).

[8] Hufbauer and Adler, *Overseas Manufacturing Investments,* pp. 70–71. Thus, when we selected our cases, one might have concluded that our results would be biased in the direction of obtaining an unfavorable effect of U.S. foreign direct investment, because our proportion of cases in less-developed countries—four out of nine—is higher than the average of all U.S. foreign direct investment in manufacturing.

Our cases differ substantially from this hypothesis. The reason for this variance is that Hufbauer and Adler assumed that in less-developed countries U.S. firms compete with local firms. In fact, we found that in less-developed countries U.S. firms compete principally with the local subsidiaries of multinational enterprises headquartered in other advanced countries.[9] This competition, combined with a high degree of protection for the local market due to very high trade barriers ranging from 55 percent to 136 percent of product value in our cases, causes us to hypothesize that the reverse classical assumptions are just as likely to apply to less-developed as to developed countries. (It must be remembered that under the reverse classical assumptions, if the U.S. firm does not invest, a foreign firm will.) And in the case of Canada, where U.S. firms control a disproportionately large share of the market and trade barriers often are not prohibitive, the reverse classical assumptions are probably less likely to apply than in less-developed countries. (That is, a U.S. investment in Canada is more likely to substitute for U.S. exports than a U.S. foreign investment elsewhere is likely to substitute for U.S. exports.) The results of our nine cases are consistent with these ideas— the estimated balance-of-payments recoupment periods average four years for our cases in less-developed countries, four years for developed countries other than Canada, and eight years for Canada.[10]

---

[9] Our finding is consistent with other studies; see Robert B. Stobaugh, et al., *The Likely Effects on the U.S. Economy of Eliminating the Deferral of U.S. Income Tax on Foreign Earnings* (Cambridge, Mass.: Management Analysis Center, 745 Concord Avenue, 1973), Chapter 2. An update of this study will be available from the Financial Executives Research Foundation (New York) in 1976.

[10] The reader is reminded that we have only four cases for less-developed countries, three cases for developed countries other than Canada, and two cases for Canada.

If there is little difference between less-developed and developed countries concerning the appropriateness of the classical and reverse classical assumptions, the question arises as to which set of assumptions our results support. The answer is clear. Our results are more consistent with the reverse classical assumptions. In only two of the nine cases—electronics in Taiwan and tires in Canada—did the output of the U.S.-owned plant abroad substitute for U.S. output. And the periods over which substitution takes place are limited to about five years. In an effort to determine where our average results lie along the spectrum between the two extreme positions (classical and reverse classical), we made a bold assumption: that each of our nine cases was representative of the industry in which it took place. Based on that assumption, the amount of the substitution for U.S. production by U.S.-owned plants abroad is equal to the sales of the foreign subsidiaries of each industry group appropriately weighted by the substitution occurring in that group. Substitution is zero in all industries except electrical machinery and rubber, and here it is substantial the first year of the investment and dwindles to zero by the end of the fifth year. The weighting of our production substitution by the sales of the appropriate industry gives the production-substitution profile for all U.S.-owned manufacturing abroad.[11] (See top of page 198.)

When these values are applied to U.S.-owned manufacturing output abroad in 1970, the result is an estimate that only 2.3 percent of U.S.-owned production abroad substi-

---

[11] More details are quoted in Piero Telesio, "The Effect of U.S. Foreign Direct Investment in Manufacturing on the U.S. Balance of Payments and U.S. Employment," Part I, pp. 4, 16, of Robert B. Stobaugh, Piero Telesio, and Jose de la Torre, Jr., *The Effect of U.S. Foreign Direct Investment in Manufacturing on the U.S. Balance of Payments, U.S. Employment and Changes in Skill Composition of Employment,* Occasional Paper No. 4, Center for Multinational Studies, Washington, D.C., February 1973.

Year of Operation	Percent of U.S.-owned production abroad that:	
	Substitutes for U.S. exports	*Does not substitute for U.S. exports*
1	12.5	87.5
2	8.2	91.8
3	4.0	96.0
4	1.4	98.6
5	0.4	99.6
6	0	0

tuted for U.S. production (this was 12.5 percent of the production generated by investments initially operated in 1970, 8.2 percent of the production generated by investments initially operated in 1969, and so on, so that none of the investments initially operated in 1965 displaced U.S. production in 1970).

The bold assumption that each of our nine cases is representative of the industry in which it occurred is both an assumption and clearly daring. Substitution is understated because surely some of the foreign production displaces U.S. production in each of the seven industries in which we found no substitution. But substitution is also overstated since almost surely the large amount that we estimate to have existed in the early years of the electronics and tire cases does not represent an average case for these industries.

Although we feel somewhat secure about our estimates of displacement for the nine cases themselves, we do not know how representative are the estimates that 12.5 percent of the foreign output displaces U.S. output the first year of operation of the foreign facility and that an average of 2.3 percent of the total U.S.-owned output abroad substitutes for U.S. output. This is an area that deserves much more research if our knowledge about the effects of U.S. foreign direct investment on the U.S. economy is to be increased.

Other trade flows also have an important effect on the U.S. balance of payments: U.S. exports of capital equipment, U.S. exports of parts and components, other U.S. exports, U.S. imports, and U.S. receipts of royalties and fees. A discussion of each category seems worthwhile.

U.S. Exports of Capital Equipment

Our estimates of what occurred *with* the U.S. investments are surprisingly similar to Hufbauer and Adler's: for our nine cases, we estimate U.S. exports of capital equipment as 21.4 percent of plant and equipment expenditures, and they estimate 27 percent, which they say "almost certainly" overstates such U.S. exports.[12]

But in the case of *no* U.S. investment, our estimates deviate dramatically from Hufbauer and Adler's. They estimate that if U.S. firms had not invested abroad, then the foreign firms making the investment would have imported 88 percent as much capital equipment as did the U.S.-owned subsidiaries; thus, U.S. exports would have been reduced by 12 percent (Table 8-3). In contrast, our case analyses indicate that virtually all of the U.S. exports of capital equipment would have been lost if the U.S. firms had not invested abroad. Such a big difference justifies a detailed explanation.

Hufbauer and Adler assumed that the import behavior of all non-U.S.-owned manufacturing firms outside the United States, in the aggregate, is representative of the

---

[12] Hufbauer and Adler, *Overseas Manufacturing Investments*, p. 23.

TABLE 8-3

EFFECT OF U.S. FOREIGN DIRECT INVESTMENT ON U.S. EXPORTS
OF CAPITAL EQUIPMENT

Line	Situation	*U.S. exports of capital equipment (as a percentage of plant and equipment expenditures by U.S. foreign affiliates in manufacturing, unless otherwise noted)*	
		Hufbauer-Adler estimates for all U.S.-owned manufacturing abroad, reverse classical assumptions[a]	*Average of nine cases, this study*
1	With U.S. investments	27.0	21.4
2	Without U.S. investments	23.8	.8
3	Loss if U.S. investments not made	3.2	20.6
4	Loss as a percentage of exports with investments (Line 3 as a percentage of Line 1)	12	96[b]

[a] Hufbauer and Adler, *Overseas Manufacturing Investments and the Balance of Payments* (Washington, D.C.: U.S. Treasury Department, 1968), pp. 22, 24.
[b] The average of the "percentage of loss" calculated for each of the nine cases is 94.

import behavior of the competitors of the foreign affiliates of U.S. multinational enterprises. Hufbauer and Adler's estimates, therefore, were based mostly on the import behavior of locally owned firms, which account for the bulk of capital goods imports. Yet in seven of our nine cases, no local firm was a serious challenge to the U.S. multinational enterprises. In the remaining two cases—paper in Canada and tractors in Europe—the principal foreign competitors were both local firms and non-U.S. multinational enterprises. Our results are strikingly similar to those of another study showing that in 59 competitive situations involving foreign affiliates of U.S. firms, a strictly local firm had the largest market share in only 12 percent of the cases.[13]

The propensity of foreign-owned enterprises to purchase equipment from their home country has been recognized for some time. An example is the explanation of conditions surrounding Britain's North Sea oil: "So long as most of the engineering design work is carried out by U.S. or Continental contractors, then there will be a natural bias towards American or other equipment, and British companies will have trouble gaining the necessary expertise in offshore work."[14]

Our case studies barely scratch the surface on this subject, but the principal author's previous experience as an engineer and discussions with business executives leads to the belief that executives see lesser risk and uncertainty in purchasing capital goods from their home country than from other countries. First, there often is a language difference, and though this can partially be offset by incurring translation costs, there is still a residual risk that some mistake will be caused by the differences in language. Second, dealing with new suppliers brings another set of risks. Questions arise. How good is the delivery promise? Will the equipment produce the products with the correct

---

[13] Stobaugh, et al., *The Likely Effects on the U.S. Economy of Eliminating the Deferral of U.S. Income Tax on Foreign Earnings*, p. 14.

[14] Adrian Hamilton, "Why Britain is Losing the Big North Sea Orders," *The Financial Times*, August 23, 1973, p. 18.

quality? Will the equipment produce at the required output? Third, there is an exchange risk, which of course often can be overcome by buying protection in the forward market; but, in that case, the risk still appears as a cost.

Other costs are incurred, too, in searching for the new suppliers, in extra travel and telephoning, and in delivery delays due to the extra time required for drawings and specifications to be transferred from vendor to purchaser and back.

Hufbauer and Adler hypothesized that when U.S. firms first go abroad they tend to buy all their capital equipment from U.S. sources, but once established, they may adopt the purchasing habits of "native firms." They noted that "the available data, however, does not permit investigation of this, or other, interesting hypotheses."[15] If in this hypothesis Hufbauer and Adler equated "native firms" with the competitors of U.S.-owned foreign subsidiaries, as they apparently do, then our cases do not support their hypothesis. All of the firms that we studied had considerable foreign experience yet they did not have the same purchasing habits as their principal competitors.

Clearly a subject for more explicit research is the purchasing pattern of U.S. affiliates in obtaining their capital equipment compared with the pattern of their chief competitors.

U.S. Exports of Parts and Components

Analyses of the nine cases in this study show a larger export of parts and components to U.S. foreign affiliates than does the Hufbauer-Adler study, 7.8 percent of affiliates' sales versus 4.2 percent. But this estimate is not

---

[15] Hufbauer and Adler, *Overseas Manufacturing Investments*, p. 23.

very important, for the U.S. Department of Commerce publishes data on exports to foreign affiliates by their parents and therefore the recorded amounts for a number of years can be determined.[16] The key question is, what would these flows have been if American firms had *not* expanded abroad? Hufbauer and Adler estimated that, in effect, a loss equal to only 17 percent of the actual U.S. exports to U.S.-owned foreign affiliates would have occurred if U.S. firms had no manufacturing facilities abroad. The results obtained from our case studies indicate that a much higher share of the exports would have been lost— some 60 to 88 percent, depending on the method of calculation used (Table 8-4). If Hufbauer and Adler are too low in their estimates, it is probably because of their assumptions about the nature of the competition U.S. firms faced abroad. As in the case of capital equipment, they ignored any special ties that foreign subsidiaries are likely to have with their parents.

Other U.S. Exports

These exports consist of goods which are not capital equipment, parts, or components, but are nevertheless closely linked with the investment. For example, there are exports made in anticipation of starting a foreign affiliate, and there are exports of products for which sales are made because of the existence of the affiliate—so-called "associated exports." The results in our nine cases do not

---

[16] For 1962–1964, see Samuel Pizer and Frederick Cutler, "U.S. Exports to Foreign Affiliates," *Survey of Current Business* (December 1965), pp. 12–16; for 1965, see Marie T. Bradshaw, "U.S. Exports to Foreign Affiliates of U.S. Firms," *Survey of Current Business* (May 1969), pp. 34–51; and for 1966 and 1970, see Betty L. Barker, "U.S. Foreign Trade Associated with U.S. Multinational Companies," *Survey of Current Business* (December 1972), pp. 20–28.

TABLE 8-4

EFFECT OF U.S. FOREIGN DIRECT INVESTMENT ON U.S. EXPORTS
OF PARTS AND COMPONENTS

Line	Situation	U.S. exports of parts and components (as a percentage of sales of U.S. foreign affiliates in manufacturing, unless otherwise noted)	
		Hufbauer-Adler estimates for all U.S.-owned manufacturing abroad, reverse classical assumptions[a]	*Average of nine cases, this study*
1	With U.S. investments	4.2	7.8
2	Without U.S. investments	3.5	3.1
3	Loss if U.S. investments not made	.7	4.7
4	Loss as a percentage of exports with investments (Line 3 as a percentage of Line 1)	17	60[b]

[a] Hufbauer and Adler, *Overseas Manufacturing Investments and the Balance of Payments* (Washington, D.C.: U.S. Treasury Department, 1968), pp. 25, 28.
[b] The average of the "percentage of loss" calculated for each of the nine cases is 88.

deviate substantially from the Hufbauer-Adler projections; we estimate these exports to be the equivalent of 2.9 percent of the total sales of the foreign affiliates, whereas Hufbauer and Adler estimate 2.3 percent.[17]

[17] Calculated from Table 3-21 of Hufbauer and Adler, *Overseas Manufacturing Investments*, pp. 31, 46.

U.S. *Imports*

Our results are diametrically opposite the Hufbauer-Adler estimates. Whereas we estimate that U.S. imports are lower *with* U.S. foreign direct investment than *without* such investment, they believe that U.S. imports are higher *with* U.S. foreign direct investment than *without* (Table 8-5). The

TABLE 8-5
EFFECT OF U.S. FOREIGN DIRECT INVESTMENT ON U.S. IMPORTS

		U.S. imports (as a percentage of sales of U.S. foreign affiliates in manufacturing, unless otherwise noted)	
Line	*Situation*	*Hufbauer-Adler estimates for all U.S.-owned manufacturing abroad, reverse classical assumptions*[a]	*Average of nine cases, this study*
1	With U.S. investments	4.3	11.2
2	Without U.S. investments	3.7	12.5
3	Drop in U.S. imports if U.S. investment not made	.6	−1.3
4	Drop as a percentage of imports with U.S. investments (Line 3 as a percentage of Line 1)	14	−12

[a] Hufbauer and Adler, *Overseas Manufacturing Investments and the Balance of Payments* (Washington, D.C.: U.S. Treasury Department, 1968), pp. 31–32.

divergence in our estimates again stems from their assumption that the behavior of all non-U.S. firms can be aggregated and taken as a proxy for the competitors of U.S. firms abroad.

U.S. Receipts of Royalties and Fees

Our cases show a slightly higher level than do the Hufbauer-Adler estimates (1.59 percent of sales versus 1.23 percent). But we estimate, and Hufbauer and Adler assume, that if U.S. foreign direct investment did not exist, the loss in U.S. receipts would approximate an amount virtually equal to all such fees (Table 8-6).

Direct Financial Flows

The financial flows that result from trade flows are the most important category affecting the balance of payments; yet direct financial flows, such as capital outflows and inflows and dividends, can also be important. Indeed, in four of our nine cases these flows were more important than the trade flows.

Because various studies have focused on the financial management of multinational enterprises[18] and considerable data are available concerning financial flows between the U.S. parent and its foreign affiliates,[19] we skip lightly over the subject, commenting only when our results differ from Hufbauer and Adler's basic assumptions that affect their balance-of-payments analyses.

Hufbauer and Adler based their main analyses on the assumption that a restriction on U.S. outflows of capital

---

[18] Sidney M. Robbins and Robert B. Stobaugh, *Money in the Multinational Enterprise* (New York: Basic Books, 1973).

[19] For example, see Leonard A. Lupo, "U.S. Investment Abroad in 1972," *Survey of Current Business* (September 1973), pp. 20–34.

TABLE 8-6

EFFECT OF U.S. FOREIGN DIRECT INVESTMENT ON U.S. RECEIPTS
OF ROYALTIES AND FEES

Line	Situation	*U.S. receipts of royalties and fees (as a percentage of sales of U.S. foreign affiliates in manufacturing, unless otherwise noted)*	
		Hufbauer-Adler estimates for all U.S.-owned manufacturing abroad, reverse classical assumptions[a]	*Average of nine cases, this study*
1	With U.S. investments	1.23	1.59
2	Without U.S. investments	0	.03[b]
3	Loss if U.S. investments not made	1.23	1.56
4	Loss as a percentage of receipts with investments (Line 3 as a percentage of Line 1)	100	98[c]

[a] Hufbauer and Adler, *Overseas Manufacturing Investments and the Balance of Payments* (Washington, D.C.: U.S. Treasury Department, 1968), p. 29.

[b] This figure means that if U.S.-owned manufacturing abroad did not exist, foreign-owned enterprises would pay additional royalties and fees equivalent to .03 percent of the actual sales of U.S. foreign affiliates in manufacturing.

[c] The average of the "percentage of loss" calculated for each of the nine cases is 99.

would not change the mix of financial resources used abroad by U.S. affiliates; that is, the historical ratio of U.S. capital to foreign capital would not be changed.[20] But they relaxed this assumption to explore the question: If an opportunity exists to substitute foreign debt for U.S. capital but is not used, what are the balance-of-payments effects? Since the cost of borrowing abroad is less than the return on U.S. foreign investment, their conclusions indicated that an expansion abroad based on a high proportion of borrowed funds would show a shorter recoupment period than a similar expansion based on a low proportion of borrowed funds. In contrast, our nine cases fail to show a clear cause-and-effect relationship between the balance-of-payments recoupment periods and the share of project funds raised abroad (Table 8-7).

*   *   *   *   *

In sum, our findings that U.S. firms typically must invest abroad if they are to serve the markets serviced by the foreign plants are consistent with the Hufbauer-Adler reverse classical assumptions. However, one difference stated earlier in this chapter emerges as being quite important: Hufbauer and Adler assumed that U.S. firms investing abroad compete primarily with local firms and that the aggregate behavior of local firms was an adequate proxy for the behavior of the foreign competitors of U.S. firms. We, on the other hand, found in our nine cases that U.S. firms abroad were competing primarily with local subsidiaries of non-U.S.-owned multinational enterprises, their behavior being quite different from that of an aggregate of local firms. Thus, we derived a recoupment period of some five and one half years compared with Hufbauer and Adler's eight and one

---

[20] Hufbauer and Adler, *Overseas Manufacturing Investments*, pp. 6, 59, and Chapter 2.

TABLE 8-7

ESTIMATED RECOUPMENT PERIODS COMPARED WITH SHARE OF
PROJECT FUNDS RAISED ABROAD, NINE CASES

	Balance-of-payments recoupment period		Portion of project funds raised abroad	
Case	*(years)*	*Rank*	*(percent)*	*Rank*
Tractors in Europe	0	1	43	4
Paper in Canada	2	2	100	8
Vehicles in Asiana	3	3½	45	5
Food in East Africa	3	3½	100	8
Electronics in Taiwan	4	5	18	2
Oil in Ireland	6	6½	0	1
Fabricated metals in Andina	6	6½	50	6
Chemicals in Japan	9	8	41	3
Tires in Canada	16	9	100	8
Average	5		55	

SOURCE: Chapters 2 through 7, this book.

half years, the difference being due mainly to the following points:

(1) The reverse classical assumptions are just as likely to apply in less-developed countries as in developed ones. *The reason:* Non-U.S. multinational enterprises operate in less-developed countries and are more capable than local firms of investing to serve markets serviced by U.S. subsidiaries if U.S. firms do not make the investment to serve such markets.

(2) Foreign investment by U.S. firms generates much larger exports of U.S. capital equipment than would exist without such investment. *The reason:* The non-U.S. multinational enterprises, with equipment suppliers in their own home countries, have a much lower propensity to buy

equipment from U.S. equipment suppliers than do either U.S. multinational enterprises or local firms.

(3) Foreign investment by U.S. firms generates much larger exports of U.S.-made parts and components than would exist without such investment. *The reason:* Non-U.S. multinational enterprises have a high propensity to supply their foreign subsidiaries from factories in their home country, just as U.S. multinational enterprises have a high propensity to supply their foreign subsidiaries from the United States.

(4) Foreign investment by U.S. firms results in a lower volume of imports into the United States than would exist without such investment. *The reason:* U.S. firms, forced through competition into investing abroad for importation of parts and components into the United States, are more likely to provide some U.S. parts and components and perform assembly work in the United States than are non-U.S. firms, which are more likely to import a completed product into the United States.

Thus, our analyses, framed to test the assumptions of Hufbauer and Adler, yield still another set of assumptions, which we hope will be subjected in turn to testing by others.

9

The Nine Cases in Perspective

> In most practical decision problems it is necessary to rely on somewhat inconclusive evidence.[1]

OF COURSE IT WOULD BE CONVENIENT for U.S. policy-makers to have conclusive evidence on the effects of U.S. foreign direct investment on the U.S. economy. But such is not the case. In the prior chapter, we reviewed in some detail Hufbauer and Adler's attempt at modeling the balance-of-payments effects of U.S. foreign direct investments; subsequent economic modeling efforts have served primarily to highlight the difficulties encountered in reaching definite conclusions with that approach.

In order to fit the complexities of the real world into the relatively few variables that can be handled in an economic model, researchers are forced into a number of simplifying assumptions. First of all, they have to decide, more or less

---

[1] William J. Fellner, "The Progress-Generating Sector's Claim to High Priority," in National Science Foundation, *Research and Development and Economic Growth/Productivity,* Papers and Proceedings of a Colloquium (Washington, D.C.: U.S. Government Printing Office, December 1971), p. 37.

arbitrarily, which firms to lump together as if they were homogeneous. This profoundly affects all that follows. They have to assume that the dynamic effects of foreign direct investment on the efficiency levels of the home and host countries are inconsequential; that local firms sell products in their home markets that are identical to those made and sold by U.S.-owned subsidiaries abroad; and that exports of intermediate goods from U.S. parents to their subsidiaries can be treated as though they are exports to unaffiliated parties.[2] These are unrealistic assumptions, and a model that uses such assumptions might well produce implausible results. For example, the output of a recent econometric study seemed to show that multinational enterprises do not receive the benefits of economies of scale in their operations and that multinational enterprises attempt to minimize profits—the econometricians who did the study recognized that this last conclusion is implausible.[3] Furthermore, the outcome of a model depends on the level of aggregation of the data used by the model builder.[4]

Given such results from leading econometricians, policymakers dealing with the effects of U.S. foreign investment likely will be forced to rely on somewhat inconclusive evidence for quite some time. Although the nine cases in this book are intended to help policymakers in

---

[2] This list is from an article by two of the leading econometricians; see Michael Adler and Guy V.G. Stevens, "The Trade Effects of Direct Investment," *The Journal of Finance* (May 1974), pp. 655-676.

[3] Ibid.

[4] Another leading econometrician (Thomas Horst) found what business executives and government officials have long believed. Tariffs imposed by a foreign country encourage U.S. firms to substitute subsidiary production for U.S. exports. The results are statistically significant at the two-digit level but not at the three-digit level. See Dale Orr's comment on Horst's work in "The Industrial Composition of U.S. Exports and Subsidiary Sales to the Canadian Market: Comment," *American Economic Review* (March 1975), pp. 230-234; and Horst's "Reply" in the same issue on page 235.

reaching a judgment, the cases should be viewed as one piece of evidence to be combined with other available pieces. The situation is similar to a search for oil. Even though a lot can be learned about surveys over a broad area, a few deep wells provide vital information—and our cases were intended to serve as the "deep wells."

The value of the nine cases comes not so much from nine situations per se as from the fact that the central conclusion we drew—U.S. firms with foreign manufacturing facilities would eventually lose the market served by their foreign plants if the firms had not built the foreign plants—is consistent with other analyses using a different methodology. For example, industry data published with the summary of our nine cases in 1972 are generally consistent with this conclusion. They depict the gradual loss over time of the economic position by the United States within any one industry or subindustry. Ninety of 119 observations of measures of U.S. competitiveness for an industry or subindustry (production in the United States as a percentage of world production, production worldwide by U.S. firms as a percentage of world production, U.S. exports as a percentage of world exports, and U.S. net trade balance) were consistent with this theme.[5] Raymond Vernon mentions a number of studies in his *Sovereignty at Bay,* including a study of a sample of nine representative chemicals (this study was made by the principal author of this book).[6] In this study, it was found that no firm, either U.S. or non-U.S., made a foreign direct investment until a foreign company had commenced man-

---

[5] Robert B. Stobaugh, et al., "U.S. Multinational Enterprises and the U.S. Economy," in Bureau of International Commerce, U.S. Department of Commerce, *The Multinational Corporation,* Volume I (Washington: Superintendent of Documents, 1972), Exhibit 4.

[6] Raymond Vernon, *Sovereignty at Bay* (New York: Basic Books, 1971), Chapter 3.

ufacture of the product. In other words, the original producer always built the first plant in its own home country and
always supplied the world market from this plant until a
foreign competitor started production outside the original
producer's home country. This study covered the entire
universe of manufacturing facilities for those products (350
worldwide) and the entire history of the products (some 60
years).

A summary of our nine cases was published in 1972 to help
policymakers at that time. In preparing this summary, we
relied on variegated evidence of this sort when we estimated
that in 1970 U.S. foreign direct investment in manufacturing
resulted in perhaps 600,000 U.S. jobs and had a positive effect
of $3 billion or more on the U.S. balance of payments; the
methodology used to obtain these estimates is presented
elsewhere.[7]

Of course, the key factor in determining these results is the
estimate that only 2.3 percent of U.S.-owned production
abroad substitutes for U.S. production, as reported in Chapter 8. However, we found that this factor could be increased
dramatically before these positive effects would become
negative. The degree of export displacement would have to
be *17* times our estimate to bring about a negative U.S.
employment effect, and *11* times our estimate to bring about
a negative effect on the U.S. balance of payments. Thus, the
likelihood seems high that the net effects indeed are positive.
Still, the caveat that accompanied our estimates in 1972
holds today (1975): Any estimate of the number of jobs or
amount of balance of payments dependent on foreign direct

---

[7] See Piero Telesio, "The Effect of U.S. Foreign Investment in Manufacturing on the U.S. Balance of Payments and Employment," in Robert B. Stobaugh,
Piero Telesio, and Jose de la Torre, Jr., *The Effect of U.S. Foreign Direct
Investment in Manufacturing on the U.S. Balance of Payments, U.S. Employment, and Changes in the Composition of Employment,* Occasional Paper No.
4, Center for Multinational Studies (Washington, D.C., February 1973), Part I.

investment must be based more on judgment than on the results of empirical tests, and no one should claim that any such estimates are accurate.[8] Therefore, we discuss the subject no further in this book. Instead, we focus in the remaining pages on the subject that likely will turn out to be the most important result of U.S. foreign direct investment—changes in the skill level and income level of the U.S. work force.

It is now recognized that foreign direct investment enables an enterprise to make more profitable use of its technology, marketing knowledge, and other tangible and intangible assets as a package than if the enterprise sold one or more of the elements separately. And, of course, the United States is the recipient of such profits attributable to foreign direct investment by U.S. enterprises.[9] But even if the United States does profit from investments abroad by U.S. firms, the redistribution effects caused within the United States are uncertain. But one thing is sure: the optimal way to attain any income distribution goal is never one that reduces total income available for redistribution.[10] Indeed, the optimal approach would be to maximize the nation's income and then redistribute it to the desired pattern. The federal government has shown some capability to redistribute income, with redistribution running into tens of billions of dollars yearly.

A simple economic model consisting of labor and capital in a static setting will suggest that the export of capital by U.S. multinational enterprises leaves U.S. labor with less

[8] Robert B. Stobaugh, et al., "U.S. Multinational Enterprises and the U.S. Economy," pp. 30-31.

[9] Richard E. Caves, "Effect of International Technology Transfers on the U.S. Economy," in Rolf R. Piekarz (ed.), *The Effects of International Technology Transfers on U.S. Economy* (Washington, D.C.: Superintendent of Documents, 1974), pp. 34-35.

[10] Ibid.

capital with which to work than if such exports of capital did not take place. So presumably, foreign direct investment results in relatively lower returns to labor and relatively higher returns to capital. For policy-making purposes, however, one has to go a step further and take into account the dynamic effects of U.S. foreign direct investment on the composition of the U.S. work force.

Perhaps the most important finding in our nine cases is that employment created in the United States as a result of U.S. foreign direct investment is of a higher skill level than exists on the average in U.S. manufacturing industries. We used the average of U.S. manufacturing as a base for comparison on the assumption that the U.S. jobs involved in the adjustment process associated with foreign direct investment came from the manufacturing sector. In fact, if the alternative to U.S. foreign direct investment were the protection of U.S. industries through the imposition of import duties or quotas, then the increase in skill level caused by U.S. foreign direct investment would be even greater, because labor skills in import-competing industries in the United States are lower than the average for U.S. manufacturing.[11] Furthermore, our case studies omitted an important aspect of U.S. foreign direct investment: the creation of U.S. jobs in research and development establishments in the United States.[12]

But if U.S. foreign direct investment does increase job skills and incomes in the United States, another question arises: How much does it cost to achieve this increase in

---

[11] Donald B. Keesing, Peter B. Kenen, Helen Waehrer, and Merle I. Yahr, contributors to Peter B. Kenen and Roger Lawrence, *The Open Economy: Essays on International Trade and Finance* (New York: Columbia University Press, 1968).

[12] A rough estimate of home office and research and development jobs created in the United States as a result of U.S. foreign direct investments is given in Raymond Vernon, "A Skeptic Looks at the Balance of Payments," *Foreign Policy* (Winter 1971-1972), pp. 52-65.

income? I know of no available data which enable that question to be answered, but perhaps a useful way to view the problem is to hypothesize that an employment cycle exists in the life of each of the industrial sectors (such as industries or subindustries) that together make up the U.S. manufacturing economy. Some evidence exists to support speculation that in each industrial sector total employment rises during the early part of the sector's life cycle and then falls during the latter part. This fall is caused by a combination of a slow-up of growth or even an absolute fall in demand for the products produced by the sector,[13] an increase in production efficiency,[14] and an increase in imports.[15] To define the model more precisely, we further hypothesize that U.S. foreign direct investment helps an industrial sector to gain employment during its middle stages and to lose employment in its declining stages.[16]

If normal attrition in the "old" sectors reduces the supply of labor in proportion to the fall in requirements for labor, then the relevant cost of adding persons at the middle stages of the industry's life cycle because of U.S. foreign direct investment is the cost of training. But if attrition is not sufficient to reduce labor supply to meet the requirements and workers must be moved from an "old" sector, then the relevant cost is that of retraining and relocating the displaced workers.

A simplistic view of the process is that U.S. foreign

[13] Victor Cook and Rolando Polli, "Validity of the Product Life Cycle," *Journal of Business* (October 1969), pp. 385-400.

[14] This increase in production efficiency is due both to static and dynamic scale economies; see Robert B. Stobaugh and Phillip L. Townsend, "Price Forecasting and Strategic Planning: The Case of Petrochemicals," *Journal of Marketing Research* (February 1975), pp. 19-29.

[15] Louis T. Wells, Jr. (ed.), *The Product Life Cycle and International Trade* (Boston: Division of Research, Harvard Business School, 1972).

[16] This hypothesis is consistent with the idea that U.S. foreign direct investment extends the firm's participation in a market longer than otherwise would be the case; see Raymond Vernon, *Sovereignty at Bay,* Chapter 3.

direct investment enables the sons and daughters of unskilled workers to obtain M.B.A. or Ph.D. degrees and
become managers or scientists in multinational enterprises
rather than following their parents into unskilled jobs. To be
sure, the creation of highly skilled jobs for the sons and
daughters is favorable. But to complete the picture, one
must consider the parents. And the overall results are
favorable to the extent that the parents can keep their jobs
until normal retirement, but less favorable to the extent that
the parents might lose their jobs, sometimes with a loss of
pension rights, and are forced to move to another community or to receive welfare. Policy makers are likely to benefit
more from the study of this subject than from studies dealing
with aggregate balance of payments and aggregate job
numbers.

Of course, the architects of social policy cannot always
wait for more information and more understanding. Issues
such as the readjustment needs of displaced workers
should be dealt with. But the remedies should be
fashioned in ways that recognize not only the special problems of the multinational firm but also the special values
that such firms generate for the U.S. economy. In some
cases this may mean correcting undesirable practices,
such as the firing of older workers who do not have
adequate retraining or pension benefits, by legislation affecting domestic activities. But in other cases, such as
changing the rules on the taxation of foreign income, this
may mean that U.S. actions should be coordinated with
parallel actions from other industrialized countries that
also provide a headquarters for multinational enterprises.
Otherwise, by handicapping U.S.-based enterprises in the
international race, there is a risk that we may be damaging
the very interests that are the object of the regulatory
measures, namely, the interests of the U.S. economy.

Index